Rails to the Tableland

by
R. F. ELLIS

AUSTRALIAN
RAILWAY
HISTORICAL
SOCIETY

Published by the

AUSTRALIAN RAILWAY HISTORICAL SOCIETY

QLD. DIVISION

Box 682, G.P.O. Brisbane. 4001

1976

Edited by the
Editorial & Publications Sub-Committee

National Library of Australia Card Number and ISBN
0 909937 06 0

First Printing 1976
Reprinted 1985
Reprinted August 1986
Reprinted November 1990
Produced by Pep Colour Pty Ltd, Brisbane
346 Bilsen Road, Geebung 4034.
Printed by Merino Lithographics
18 Baldock Street, Moorooka, Qld 4105

Front Cover: B15Con. class 4-6-0 No. 306 climbs around the Jungara Horseshoe with a special train in July 1

(R. Des

Inside Front Cover: Stoney Creek Bridge, probably one of the best known bridges in Australia, undergoing testin 30th June 1890. The test train consists of Baldwin built 2-6-0 construction engine "Pioneer" and a S class timber wa loaded with rails.

(G.E. Bond Collec

The driver oils the motion of B15 Con. class No. 206 at Kuranda Station about 1908.
(R.F. Ellis Collection)

Contents

Above: No. 4 Tunnel

(Cairns Historical Society, courtesy E. Ward)

Below: The Barron River Gorge about 1910-11 showing the Range Railway's route along the gorge side. On the right, a B15 class struggles past Robb's Monument with a heavy goods train for the Tableland.

(A.R.H.S. Queensland Division Collection)

The Railway to the Atherton Tableland. Approaching Redlynch

(Cairns Historical Society courtesy E. Ward)

Foreword

North Queensland is rich in history, and its residents are justifiably proud of their interesting heritage. The area developed from the early 1870s into one of the major mining areas in Australia in the years leading up to the First World War, but since then, the mining activity has declined and its place taken by primary industry, mainly cattle, tobacco and sugar cane. Cairns, basking in its tropical splendour, and after somewhat doubtful beginnings, has expanded to become one of the major cities of the North.

As in other areas, the railway played an important part in the development of the surrounding country, and the "iron horse" quickly established itself as the most reliable means of transport in the golden years prior to the introduction of the internal combustion engine and the conquest of the air. Today, the railway is considered by many people to be outmoded, however in Queensland, and especially in the North, it still has an important role to play.

The Cairns Railway has grown with this development as one of Australia's northernmost rail outposts, and its Range Railway has quickly established itself into one of Queensland's major tourist attractions. This then, is the story of the Cairns Railway, and is dedicated to those hardy pioneering men and women who, a centry ago, made a dream into a reality.

Ray Ellis, Brisbane, 1976

Above: Bullock teams were used extensively prior to the advent of the railway. Here a team is being used to snig timber for the railway construction.

(Cairns Historical Society, courtesy E. Ward)

Below: Clearing a watercourse near No. 1 Tunnel during the construction period.

(Cairns Historical Society, courtesy E. Ward)

How It All Began . . .

Probably the first questions that the traveller on a train up the Cairns Range will ask would be "Why was it built?", "Why was it built from Cairns to the Atherton Tableland?", "Why not from Cardwell, Innisfail, Gordonvale, Port Douglas or Mossman?" Surely in the 1880's, the Government of the day did not build it as a scenic attraction for the thousands of tourists who now travel over the line!!

To uncover the complete story of the decision to build the railway via the famous Barron Gorge, we must look back to 1871. Although inland pastoral and mining settlement were being pioneered, pushing northward from Charters Towers, up until 1871 only sketchy information had been provided of the area of coastline north of Cardwell. Some Naval ships had casually inspected Green Island and Trinity Bay, and in particular, the "Rattlesnake", under Capt. Owen Stanley, reported a wide creek at Trinity Bay. However the first definite knowledge of the coast from Cardwell northward was gathered when the paddle steamer cruiser, H.M.S. "Basilisk", under Capt. Moresby, followed a route inside the Barrier Reef in 1871 and took on food and water at Fitzroy Island. On its return trip in 1872, the "Basilisk" used Fitzroy Island as its base to search for the survivors of the wrecked brig "Maria". Again in 1873, the same vessell captured two schooners for alleged breaches of the Imperial Pacific Islanders Protection Act and took them to Fitzroy Island. It was whilst engaged in these occurrences, that the vessel was able to make fairly accurate surveys of the coastline, and in particular Trinity Bay, which in part, was described as "a low lying shore with mud and mangrove".

The discovery of the Palmer Goldfields in 1873 and James Mulligan's report of payable gold on the field led to the desireability of easy access to the sea. G.E. Dalrymple was appointed to take charge of an expedition from Cardwell in September 1873 and made ascents of the Johnstone, Russell and Mulgrave Rivers, and viewed and inspected Trinity Bay inlet. He pushed on and reached the Endeavour River where he met the S.S. "Leichardt" with a Government party onboard. Cooktown thus became established as the port and base of the Palmer Goldfields. West of Cardwell lay the Etheridge Goldfields and access by road was from Cardwell, via the Seaview Range. There was therefore two goldfields with two very slow dray roads giving access to the sea.

In the meantime, beche-de-mer fishermen, using Cooktown as a base, were working further south, and by camping on Green Island and Fitzroy Island, added to the knowledge of Trinity Bay. Timber-getters were also moving south from Cooktown, first to the Bloomfield and Daintree Rivers, and later to exploit the rich forests of cedar on the Mossman, Barron and Mulgrave Rivers. Then in 1876, J.V. Mulligan made the discovery of the Hodgkinson Goldfield, directly west of the then little known Trinity Bay, and as a result man flocked to it. Until this time, although the coast between Cardwell and Cooktown had become known to the beche-de-mer-fishermen and timber-getters, its dense scrub and uncivilised aborigines prevented anything like complete exploration and settlement. Amongst these early venturers was a man with the name of Bill Smith.

Access to the new Hodgkinson Field was from Cooktown, via the Palmer River, a very rough and slow trip, or by a track from the Field which linked up with the Cardwell-Etheridge road, the distance this way being some 139 miles, and therefore costs of transport were heavy indeed. In June 1876, rumours were rife on the Hodgkinson Field following the belated publication of Dalrymple's report of a fine new harbour at Trinity Bay. Bill Smith, now on the field, journeyed with a party to find a short route to the sea, but they were stopped by dense scrub country. However from the heights, they had obtained a view of the sea, and Smith definately recognised Trinity Bay. He was enthusiastic about the advantages of the inlet and the fine depth of water to be found there. Meanwhile, the Government sent a Mr. Sheridan, Police Magistrate at Cardwell, to Trinity Bay to fully inspect the harbour and he selected a site for a settlement which he named "Thornton". Bill Smith was sent by a Thornborough Committee on the Hodgkinson Field to Cooktown, thence by boat to Trintiy Bay, from where he tackled the ranges, though not by the then unknown Barron River Gorge. Returning to Trinity Bay, he ascended the range again, and pushed through to Thornborough, doing the 70 mile journey in about four days. Two days previous to Smith's departure, another party led by Sub-Inspector Douglas left Thornborough and taking a new route, followed the divide of the Surprise and Stoney Creeks, came down at the foot of Glacier Rock, and arrived at the Inlet about the same time that Smith arrived at Thornborough. Thus it was, that whilst Smith

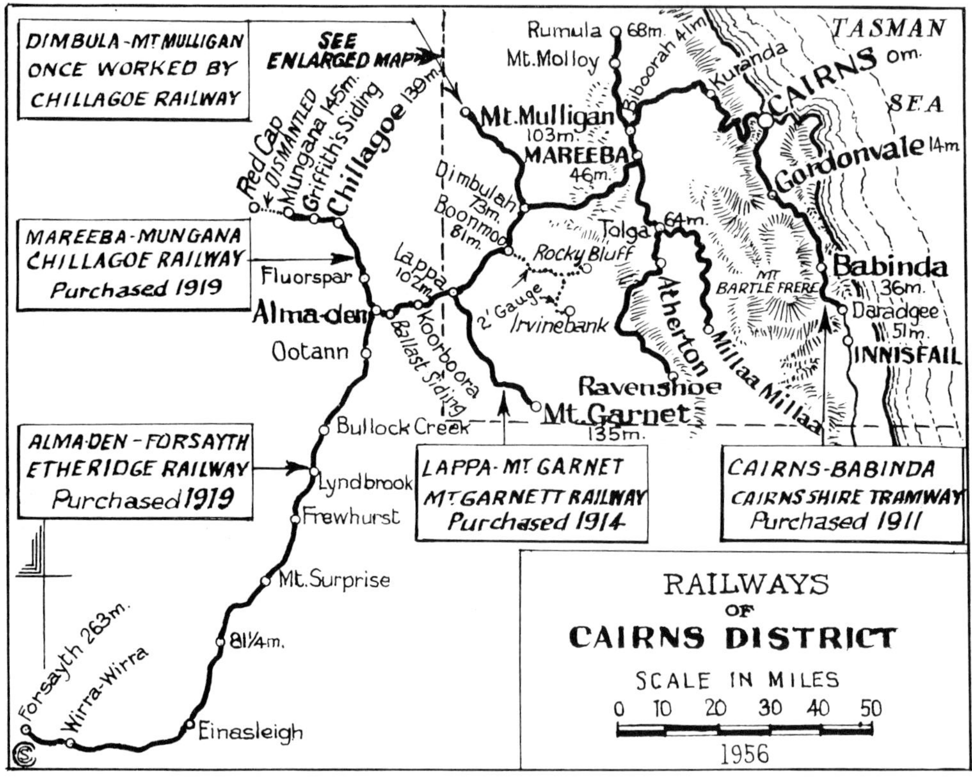

found a route up the range, Douglas found a different route down the range. Douglas met Sub-Inspectors Johnstone and Townsend at the Inlet, who had arrived in the pilot boat from Cardwell, and it was these men who patrolled the area and discovered the river north of the inlet which they named the Barron after the Chief of Police.

It was then realised that Trinity Bay could be used as a port for the Hodgkinson Goldfields and in very short time, three hundred people had settled at Trinity Bay; miners and others at Smiths Landing, and the official party at the end of the beach at the mouth of the Inlet. Althouth Sheridan had named the place Thornton, Commissioner Sharkey was sent from Townsville on the "Porpoise" to survey the place for a town, and it was he who officially named it after the new Governor of Queensland—Cairns. The official party landed from the "Porpoise" on 6th. October, 1876 and the commencing peg of the new town was placed at the corner of Wharf and Abbott Streets.

A dray road, in the place of the tracks found by Smith and Douglas, was needed as both routes were reported to be bad by experienced dray men. Following successive trials and tribulations by various pioneers, during which time Messrs. Doyle and Evans found a mighty cataract on the Barron River, Frederick Warner plotted and found a way from the goldfields which could be used as a practical dray road. This route crossed the Barron River at Biboohra, re-crossed it near Kuranda, then came down a spur three miles north of the Barron Falls, and at the bottom re-crossed the Barron River again at the top of the tidal waters—Kamerunga (Lake Placid to the tourists). During the early part of 1877, £9,979 was spent on the road, but it finally proved unsatisfactory, being very steep and needed "double banking" (using two teams for one load) to the top; even then there were numerous sharp pinches to the top and until the scrub country was passed.

One of the most colourful persons to appear in the North emerged at this time in history, and no history of the North would be complete without reference to this most extraordinary man who roamed the jungle in the infant years of the North. It is asserted that he assisted Bill Smith in his exploration from Trinity Bay, that he was with Mulligan on the Palmer; but what is true, is that his exploits became legendary. His name was Christie Palmerston. In 1877 he was prospecting at the head of the Daintree River and those who have seen this wild jungle mountainous country, even today, will acknowledge his bushcraft. Palmerston made friends with the

Above: Construction train crossing Bridge No. 11, built by John Walker & Co. Ltd., Maryborough, on the Second Section of the Range Railway, between Redlynch and Kuranda. The locomotive is ex-Great Northern Railway 2-6-0 No. 3 used during the construction period and later became part of the B11 class. Note the American styling of this Baldwin built engine.

(J.L.N. Southern Collection)

Below: The entrance to the bore for No. 1 Tunnel before the rails had been laid.

(Cairns Historical Society, courtesy E. Ward)

Above: The tunnel gang pose for their photograph at the upper end of No. 10 Tunnel.
(Cairns Historical Society, courtesy E. Ward)

Below: "Pioneer", the Baldwin engine used for the construction of the Second Section of the Range Railway with John Robb and a group of engineers, surveyors and other dignitaries on the newly completed Stoney Creek Falls Bridge.
(G. Bond Collection)

aborigines wherever he went and acquired the knowledge from them with regard to edible roots, nuts, yams, fruits and fishing grounds. In return, he was able to furnish the aborigines with game from his firearms and this enables him to roam country no other white man could penetrate. In April, 1877, Palmerston and his mate Layton discovered a track suitable as a good road from Port Douglas to the Hodgkinson Goldfield. The way was much shorter and less precipitous than the route from Cairns, and, as Port Douglas had a fine but shallow harbour, the establishment of a road to Port Douglas made it bloom and so trade consequently turned away from Cairns to Port Douglas. So much that most of the business people in Cairns and Smithfield, which had grown at the foot of Warners road, shifted their business premises from there to Port Douglas. It is pertinent to state here that Palmerston's find really led to the establishment of Port Douglas and that before it became officially proclaimed as a port of entry, it had been known as Terrigal, Port Owen, Owenville, Salisbury and Port Salisbury.

With the opening of Port Douglas, Cairns suffered a serious blow to its importance and a decline in its prosperity. The Police Magistrate was transferred from Cairns to Port Douglas in 1878 and in early 1879, the Lands Office, and then the District Court, were also transferred from Cairns. The gold escort from the Hodgkinson had in 1878 already been diverted to the new port. In June 1875, Mulligan had found good prospects of tin on the Wild River, and shortly after his Hodgkinson gold find, tin was also found near where Mareeba now stands, at Tinaroo. Thus the road from port Douglas began to serve both the Hodgkinson and Tinaroo Fields. In May 1880, about eight miles below Mulligan's find on the Wild River, a rich discovery of tin led to the Herberton Tinfields rush. The Port Douglas road was hastily pushed through to Herberton and Port Douglas boomed afresh, and Cairns began to die. Horse pack teams became the only users of the Cairns Road and the years 1880 and 1881 were the greatest depression in Cairns, relieved only mildly by the short lived Goldsborough Gold find (near Gordonvale) and timber getting. A devastating cyclone in 1879 brought total disaster to Smithfield and serious loss to Cairns, and over the years 1878 to 1881, many speeches were made in Parliament fearing the total annihilation of Cairns, and one Member even stated that the town was doomed, and that the Government should return the money paid for land on the grounds that the buyers had been misled by glaring advertisements!!

However those people who stayed on in Cairns had faith and they continued to eke out a small existence, believing that Providence would provide and see them through their various calamaties. Meantime a shorter route from Herberton to the coast was being explored, firstly John Atherton and then James Robson (later murdered by an aborigine at Myola) penetrated from Herberton through to, and down, the Mulgrave Valley, allowing tin to be packed direct from Herberton to load into small steamers at the far reaches of Trinity Inlet. The distance was much shorter than the Herberton-Port Douglas Rd. but was still only a track , and drays could not travel on it. Then came misery for the thousands of people on the Herberton Field. The road from Port Douglas was proving difficult in the wet season and in 1882 the north had a very prolonged wet season so that Herberton, unable to obtain supplies, was on the verge of famine. It was not until June of that year that supplies reached the Field, and then carried in at high prices because of the long time in transit. As a result the people of Herberton raised loud and angry voices and began agitation for a railway to the coast.

Mr. Stubley, M.L.A. for Charters Towers, visiting Herberton in January 1882 was the first to make mention of a railway, and the famine which followed certainly showed that such a need existed. Mr. Cooper, M.L.A. for Cook promised a railway to Herberton from Port Douglas. Coming general elections and cold weather in the south saw visits of leading politicians all with the promise of a railway until in March 1882, Mr. Macrossan, Minister for Works and Mines, announced, in consequence to a promise to both the people of Port Douglas and Cairns, commissioned Christie Palmerston to search for a railway route from Herberton to the coast. In February 1882 both Port Douglas and Cairns had formed a Railway League and engaged in a long and bitter fight for the railway. Meanwhile Palmerston commenced his journey at the Mossman River and tried the Mossman and Mowbray valleys and spurs in turn looking for a route. During the year, he worked along the coast from Mossman to Cairns and then tried the Barron Valley and the Mulgrave Valley. Geraldton, later to be renamed Innisfail, then came into the competition for the line, considering the claims of Mourilyan Harbour to be sound, and formed a Railway League also. Failing to get the Government to send Palmerston to find a route, the local Divisional Board (fore-runner of the Shire Council) engaged him instead.

In February 1882, Mr G. Monk, surveyor, was appointed to investigate and report on the routes being found by Palmerston. Mr. Monk was an experienced bushman, as well as surveyor, but was the first to acclaim Palmerston's marvellous superiority in the jungle clad mountainous environment. In November 1882, Palmerston made the trip from Mourilyan to

Herberton in nine days and repeatedly came across the track made by Inspector Douglas in May 1882 during the long heavy wet season. Douglas had travelled from Herberton to Mourilyan and had wired the Colonial Secretary, "Arrived Mourilyan 28th. May. Fearful trip. No chance of road. 20 days without rations, living on roots principally. 19 days rain without intermission. Brought party back safe but suffering from sores. Track marked and cut". This gave some idea of the hard and arduous trip that it must have been. In good weather, Palmerston was able to see where Douglas could have avoided the precipitious country over which he travelled and he was very enthusiastic about the route he himself had found, but the Divisional Board failed to pay him for his survey and he refused to have any further dealings with them. Palmerston only submitted his reports on the routes he had found under Government commission. In January, 1883, in heavy rain, following pressure from Geraldton, Mr. Monk, accompanied by Palmerston, made the trip from Herberton to Mourilyan, but following Palmerston's disagreement with the Board, no report was made.

In March, 1884, Mr. Monk's surveys and reports were submitted and culminated in being in favour of the route found by Palmerston via the Barron Valley gorge. The storm of indignation which followed from Port Douglas and Geraldton was as enormous as the jubilant expression from the people of Cairns. The protests were so great that Mr. O. Amos carried out several trial surveys from Port Douglas, but, nevertheless, by February 1885, Mr Monk and Mr Amos completed working plans for the Cairns—Herberton route and on 19th. September 1885, Cabinet approved of the plans. The controversy that raged thereafter over the selection of Cairns would fill several large volumes, however should anyone's interest in the matter be sufficient, it is recommended that the pamphlet, written by Swannick, which is now in the Oxley Memorial Library in Brisbane, be read.

The later opening of the line made a gateway to the rich mining belt, to the huge timber reserves and opened up immense and enduring grazing and agricultural lands. By bringing inland trade to Cairns, the port was enlarged, industry established and the town prospered. The passing of the years is adding more to the romance of Australian exploration and discovery, more particularly as the genesis of many settlements both inland and on the coast can be traced directly to inland exploration. This is true to a marked degree in North Queensland, where the coast towns from Mackay to Cooktown, with the exception of Innisfail, were founded as a result of either pastoral or mineral development inland.

Engine No. 3, after receiving its post-1889 number, 178, on Bridge No. 11 at the entrance to Tunnel No. 4, 1892.
(J.L.N. Southern Collection)

Construction Of The Cairns Range Railway.

An entralling chapter in the history of the development of North Queensland was the construction of the Range Railway—an engineering feat of tremendous magnitude achieved when North Queensland was still young. It still stands today as a monument to the splendid ambitions, fortitude and suffering of the hundreds of men who were engaged in its construction, and of those who lost their lives among the perils which this marvellous work involved.

On 10th. May 1886, the then Premier of Queensland, Sir Samuel Griffiths, used a silver spade to turn the first sod. The ceremony was performed on railway property almost directly behind where the Queens Hotel now stands and celebrations embracing almost the entire population of Cairns lasted all that day and night. The survey of the section had been commenced under Mr. Robert Ballard, then Chief Engineer of the Central & Northern Division of Queensland Railways, and was continued under Mr. Willoughby Hannam, Chief Engineer of the Northern Division, under whom the works were designed and partially constructed. The work was finally completed under Mr.T. Annett, Mr. Hannam's successor. The construction was achieved by three separate contracts for lengths of 8m. 12c., 15m. 18c. and 23m. 20c., a total length of 46m. 50c., surmounting (mainly over Section Two) the eastern face of a vast mineral-bearing and grazing tableland, leading to Mareeba. Sections One and Three were comparatively easily located and constructed, but the ascent of the tableland was very arduous due to the steep grades, the dense jungle, and the hostility of the natives. The rise began at the 7¼ mile, near Redlynch station which was 18 feet above sea level, and climbed first with a ruling gradient of 1 in 50 to the 11½ mile and thence to Stoney Creek (14½ miles) at 1 in 60, with 5 chain radius curves. The summit was reached at 19m. 10c. and an altitude of 1,073 feet above sea level, so that a total rise of 1,055 feet was achieved in 11m. 70c., or on an average of 88 feet per mile. There were three curves of less than 5 chain radius, including the 4 chain curve at Stoney Creek Bridge, and of the total length of the line, only slightly over half was straight track.

The first section of the line from Cairns ran to just beyond Redlynch and the contract for this portion was won by a Mr. P. C. Smith at a price of £20,000. However the section was dogged by bad luck and a possible lack of firm supervision. It may be interesting to recall here that to secure a job as a navvie on the project, one had to supply his own shovel! On 7th. July 1886, the "Lowther Castle" arrived at Cairns with the first shipment of 2,600 tons of rails and materials. The railway wharf had been built by Louis Severin but due to the heavy weight of the cargo, the "Lowther Castle" was drawing 21 feet and some of the cargo had to be unloaded into lighters at the fairway buoy so that the vessel could enter port—the lightering alone cost £2,000. Delay prolonged the work well into the wet season. Sickness was prevalent amongst the navvies, the working conditions in the swamps and jungles being so appalling that a Ministerial Enquiry was ordered into the deaths of two men who died through lack of medical attention. Horses used in the swamps became so hopelessly bogged that they had to be destroyed.

On 21st. January, John Robb's tender of £290,094 for the second section to Myola was accepted. By June 1887, on the first section, the rails had been laid to only a little beyond Stratford and yet by that time, John Robb, in preparing for the building of the second section, had established his offices at Barronville (later Kamerunga), had erected a sawmill and opened a ballast pit in the Barron gorge there, and had started gangs of clearing and the cuttings of the second section. P.C. Smith had relinquished his contract for the first section in November 1886 and it was taken over by McBride & Co., but they too ceased operations in January 1887. The Queensland Government then took over the completion of the first section. On 2nd. January 1887, the schooner "Silvery Wave" landed two composite carriages on the railway wharf, the first to arrive, and in March 1887, the brig "Mabel White" landed the first consignment of plant and material for John Robb's contract together with the first locomotive. The first section from Cairns to Redlynch was opened on 8th. October 1887 and shortly thereafter a temporary line to Kamerunga ballast pit and sawmill. The first railway station in Cairns was built by Reid Bros. and when the line was opened for public traffic on 26th September 1887, the train crew comprised Driver Henry Fuelling, Fireman William Bell and Guard N. Harris.

The preparatory work for the range railway proved very difficult and it was found impractical to lay dray roads along the site of the works and pack tracks had to be cut, not only at the formation level of the railway, but also down to the main Government camp at Kamerunga and

Stoney Creek Falls Bridge, 1892.

(J.L.N. Southern Collection)

the contractor's camp at Stoney Creek. Mules were found more useful than horses, so were used to transport all the plant, tools, explosives, cement, sand and plate-laying materials. The clearing of the jungle alone cost £770 per mile and did not yield much in the way of satisfactory constructional material (as happens in most cases), the only variety of timber found useful being hickory.

The work on the second section to Myola had commenced on 28th. April 1887 by gangs working on clearing cuttings, etc., by sub-contract, and it was during this work that the first fatal accident occurred. Recollections of the building over the ranges various escarpment included such sights as men being slung by ropes between Red Bluff and Camp Oven Creek as they cleared the formation. At one place there was a rough track leading above the escarpment and it was stated that many men fell to their death when traversing it. On the second section there were ninety-eight curves over the 15 mile length and bridges over every ravine and creek down the mountain side, with some of the bridges hanging

Above: Barron Falls Station from the Kuranda direction, about 1912.

(John Knowles Collection)

Below: View from above Camp Oven Creek showing the hillside laid bare during the construction. In the tropical climate, it did not take long for the slope to be covered with rich vegetation once again.

(Cairns Historical Society, courtesy E. Ward)

dizzily over depths of hundreds of feet. Robb and his men tackled the jungle and mountains, though not with bulldozers, jack hammers and other present day equipment, but with brains, fortitude, hand tools and drills, dynamite, buckets and bare hands. Great escarpments were taken from the mountain above the line and every loose rock and overhanging tree had to be carefully removed. It was during this type of operation that the famous Red Bluff and the Glacier Rock were exposed and became landmarks as the line was built around the spur leading from Stoney Creek to the Barron Gorge. During the construction, the navvies' camps were formed at every cutting and tunnel and even comparatively narrow ledges became the sites of stores, some of them not wholly catering for the needs of the men in the way of groceries and drapery!! At Number 3 tunnel, Stoney Creek, the springs at the foot of the Glacier Rock, Camp Oven Creek and Gray' Pocket (Rainbow Creek) just above the falls, were, in their day, busy and thriving townships and Kamerunga, at the foot of the range and site of John Robb's main office and sawmill, boasted no less than five hotels. At one stage of the construction, 1,500 men in all were engaged in various activities associated with the building of the line.

In September 1888, the Government intimated that it did not want to take over the temporary railway line that had been laid from Redlynch to Kamerunga and the sand pits of the Barron River. Sand from this source was used for all the concrete work on the second section. Wagons were sent up the permanent way as far as construction allowed, then the sand was bagged, packed on the mules, and taken along ledges cut in the mountain side to the different jobs. Cement, which came in casks from abroad in those days, was also taken on the mules up the mountain side from the junction of the Stoney Creek and Barron River to the springs at the Bluff. The building of the longest tunnel, No. 15, proved difficult, and in 1889 led to a temporary hold-up in construction. However on 11th. November 1889, the Chief Engineer of Railways, Mr. Stanley, and one of the three Railway Commissioners, arrived and authorised the necessary deviation from the original plans, and work recommenced on the 17 chain tunnel. To make up for lost time, drives were made so that men could work on eight faces of the tunnel at once.

Earthworks were particularly heavy, deep cuttings and extensive embankments being required, to a total volume of just over three million cubic yards. The ground was specially

Camp Oven Creek Hotel in 1888. Built by M. Boland, this establishment no doubt provided a welcome respite for the construction workers from the rigours of their arduous task.

(Cairns Historical Society, courtesy E. Ward)

treacherous in the Barron Gorge, where the average slope of the ground was 45 degrees, and the whole surface was covered with a layer of disjointed rotten rock and soil to a depth of 15 to 25 feet, Bridgework was also a major item, the total length of steel bridging on the mountain section being 800 feet, involving 339 tons of steel, whilst there was an additional 6,215 feet of wooden bridges. The steelwork was all cut, fitted and partly riveted by Walkers Ltd. of Maryborough, at a cost of £7,850, delivered at Cairns. The outstanding steel bridge was that at Stoney Creek, built on a 4 chain radius curve, with four 50'0" spans, alternating with three 30'0" tower spans with wrought iron lattice legs, end piers of concrete and approaches of timber. Extensive tunnelling was naturally required in such difficult country, and altogether, fifteen tunnels were constructed, varying in length from 56 yards to 470 yards, and totalling 1,910 yards. Some were rather complicated, for instance in No. 11 tunnel, there were 5 chain reverse curves, whilst in No. 15 tunnel (the longest of them), there was a 7½ chain curve at one end and a 15 chain curve at the other end, with a 5 chain curve in the middle!! The driving of these tunnels was all done by hand and the final cost of the completed structures was about 46 per lineal yard. The gauge of the line is of course 3'6", and as far as the 9m.6c. peg, the vignoles pattern rails were 26'0" long and weighed 41½ lbs. per yard, whilst the remainder of the line was laid with 60 lb. rail in 24'0" lengths. The gravel ballast used was obtained from the Barron riverbed at Kamerunga, a temporary branch line of 1¾ miles being laid to the pit to facilitate the transport of ballast to the track bed. Sleepers were laid at rates varying between 2,640 per mile on the straight track, to 2,880 per mile on curves, and were of hickory (obtained from the surrounding jungle) and bloodwood. The maximum speeds permitted on the sharp curves were 18 m.p.h. for passenger trains and 15 m.p.h. for mixed and goods trains.

The men employed on the construction were of various nationalities, with the majority being either Italian or Irish; the Italians coming under a special Treaty between Italy and Queensland. Mention should also be made of the Italian flag which for a few years flew unmolested during and after the construction, from Robb's Monument! It is necessary to state that many vague and inaccurate statements have been made regarding loss of life in the building of Range portion of the railway. To date, records have been found to confirm the death of twenty-three men, however, hundreds of accidents, and no doubt some deaths, mainly through carelessness with explosives, have been left unrecorded. Despite there being a resident doctor, the first was a Doctor Queely succeeded by a Dr. Dobbie at Kamerunga, by far the greatest killer of men

Glacier Rock, about 1915

(John Knowles Collection)

employed on the railway construction was sickness, caused through malaria, scrub typhus, dysentary, snake bite and scrub ticks. Kamerunga even recorded two cases of leprosy.

At a meeting held at Kamerunga on 20th. April 1888, the Irish workers were predominant in the formation of the Victorian Labour League, but there was little labour trouble between workers and contractors as all realised the magnitude of the task before them and industrial relations could be described, especially in view of what happens in this day and age, as very harmonious. In August 1890, the great maritime strike spread to the railway workers and they formed a Union, the United Sons of Toil. They made a demand of 9/- per day. By September the differences between contractors and navvies had been resolved so that the navvies received 8/6d. per day, the previous rate being 8/-, with a proportionate scale for classified skilled workers. Some further friction developed in November over the dismissal of two of the strike committee, but the men were not reinstated. The Sons of Toil decided to affiliate with the Australian Labour Federation and a Mr Lowry, the A.L.F. delegate, addressed meetings in Cairns on alien immigration, Italian

Above: Bridge No. 36, over Surprise Creek, 1892

(J.L.N. Southern Collection)

Below: Three engines, a B11 2-6-0 and two B13 4-6-0s, test the Barron River Bridge at Biboohra. Note the different style of bridge used on the Third Section to that of the Second Section.

(Cairns Historical Society, courtesy E. Ward)

Above: Landslides caused by heavy rain wreak havoc with any mountain railway and the Cairns Railway is no exception. Clearing up proceeds after such an event at the upper end of No. 11 Tunnel about 1911.
(Cairns Historical Society, courtesy E. Ward)

Below: A B13 class provides the motive power for a work train and its gang employed in clearing blocked entrance to No. 10 Tunnel after a landslide, about 1911.
(Cairns Historical Society, courtesy E. Ward)

Above: Landslides led to contruction of temporary deviation. In this instance, the deviation (man standing of the centre line at 13m 45c., since removed, employed 3 chain radius curves. The date is March 1911.
(Cairns Historical Society, courtesy E. Ward)

Below: When a landslide occured, trains were run to each side of break and passengers exchanged. This 1911 view at "The Springs" shows the passengers transfering their luggage to the waiting train.
(Cairns Historical Society, courtesy E. Ward)

labour, and generally organised labour activities.

During the construction, in the years 1888-1889, a great transformation took place in the streets of Cairns. Until then, from Abbott Street to Macleod Street was only a sandy boggy track, that area being mostly swampy mangrove. The town Council made arrangements with the railway contractors and special ballast lines were laid from the railway station down Shields Street and into Abbott Street, and railway trucks unloaded rocks and spoil from the range construction into the streets, thus commencing the first large scale reclamation of the swamps and mangroves of Cairns. On 11th. January 1890, the dredge "Platypus" arrived at Cairns to commence work on the deepening of the harbour and this was so successful that in November of that year, the barque "Comrade" from England entered the port with 5,000 barrels of cement for the Range railway without having to lighter part of her cargo

On 28th. April 1890, His Excellency the Governor, General Sir Henry Norman made the second vice-regal visit to Cairns and he and his party made an inspection of the construction. John Robb tendered a reception to His Excellency and his party in a most unusual manner—to the unbounded astonishment of the Governor—on the Stoney Creek bridge, then under construction and nearly completed!! Planks had been laid over the sleepers on the finished portion, a handrail erected, roofed over, and a long table built along the middle part of the bridge where the rails were to be laid. No speeches were made due to the noise of the Falls, and only one toast was proposed—to the Governor. Despite its unusual location, one could almost say there was a perfect combination—the pretty falls on one side, dizzy depths on the other, splendid company, plenty of food and drink and—no speeches!! The Governor's special train arrived at the falls with the engine pushing the Governor's special carriage, and behind the engine, wagons fitted with seats for the journalists and others. Later several of the pressmen made a trip on horseback to view the mighty cateract found by Doyle and Evans—the Barron Falls. Among them were a number of Northern Queensland newspaper notables and strangely enough, a Captain Baden-Powell!

By the end of 1890, the cementing of all the tunnels was completed, platelaying was well to the top of the range and men were leaving as work on the several bridges was finished. The year 1891 commenced with an early, heavy and prolonged wet season and a heavy landslide occurred on the railway. Seventy-five inches of rain fell in six weeks, but work on the railway continued and on 9th. February, the last iron bridge was completed. On 12th. March 1891, the first ballast train reached the Barron Falls, and a

B15 class No. 42 works a ballast train across the newly completed Mervyn Creek Bridge about 1922-23 which had replaced the earlier wooden structure seen in the background.

(A.R.H.S. Queensland Division Collection)

month later on 12th. April, reached Kuranda. By 13th. May 1891, the rail was laid to the end of the second section at Myola. John Robb was refused the right to carry goods or passengers, but a month later on 15th June 1891 the railway was formerly opened by Mr. Johnston, one of the three Railway Commissioners, for goods traffic only. On 25th. June 1891, passenger traffic was commenced, and John Robb entertained a large official party at luncheon at the Barron Falls. The people of Cairns, however were annoyed that no excursion was arranged, or public holiday proclaimed, or any fuss made of the opening of the line.

John Robb is said to have made a profit of £125,000 on his contract for the second section, although it is not possible to substantiate this and one must cast grave doubts on his profit being so large. In 1892 he filed a claim with the Queensland Government for the sum of £262,311, but was later only awarded the amount of £20,000 after arbitration. John Robb did not settle in the North, but after his work had been completed, returned south to Melbourne. Robb's Monument was left as a memorial to him, and the great rock may still be seen today, standing like a sentinel, overlooking the mighty Barron River gorge.

The completion of the second section of the Cairns-Herberton Railway to Myola in 1891, five years after the first sod had been turned at Cairns, opened up an easy access by road and rail from the various centres of the hinterland to the port of Cairns. The building of the railway beyond Myola, the third section to Mareeba being under contract to Messrs Sutherland and McKenzie, is another story, however brief details of the lines on the Atherton Tableland are given elsewhere to give a general idea of the Cairns Railway. It is interesting to note that one of the first to use the new railhead at Myola was the famous coaching firm of Cobb & Co. The opening of the line spelt disaster to the town of Port Douglas, and it now rests snugly and lonely as a tourist's delight, with its pioneer buildings and other glorious points of interest. With Cardwell no longer needed as a jumping off place to the inland, it too faded into solemnity, although it has recently seen a revival through tourism. Geraldton, later Innisfail, prospered and enlarged in its own right caused by the establishment of the sugar industry, and it was to play little part in the future development of the interior.

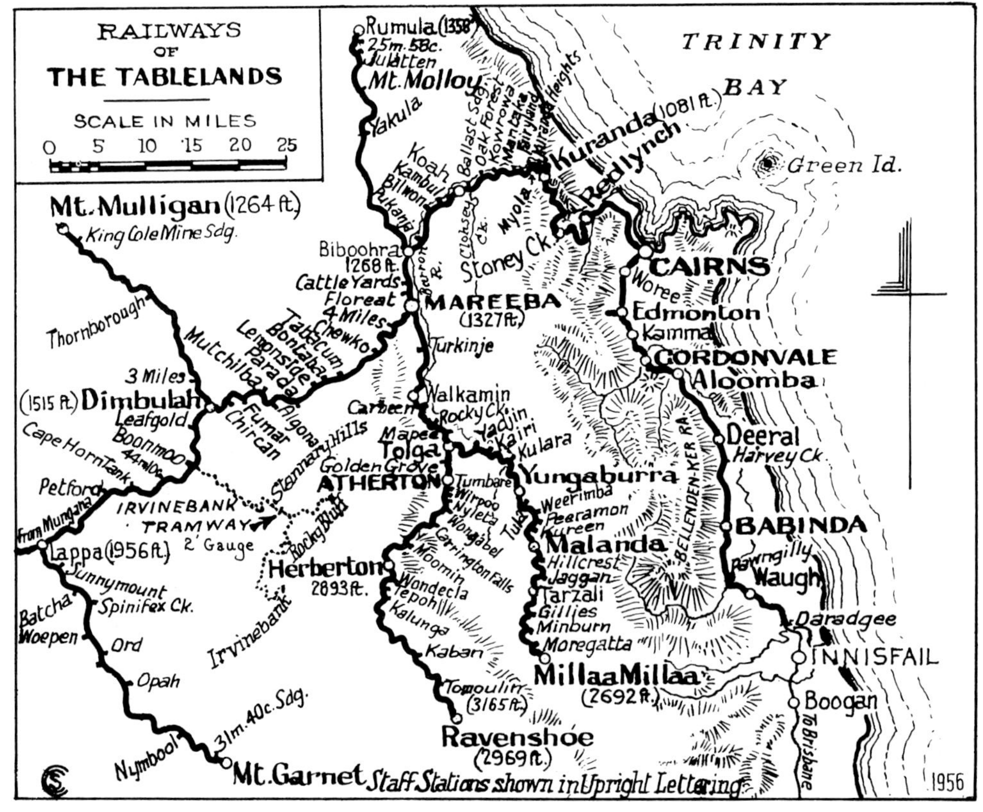

Description Of The Cairns Railway.

(Authors Note: In this description of the Cairns Railway, I have chosen to describe the line as it was in 1956. This has been done for two reasons—firstly, it has allowed me to make extensive use of the excellent description of the lines made by the well-known Australian railway historian, the late C. C. Singleton in the A.R.H.S. Bulletin in 1957, and secondly, at this time, the Cairns Railway was still intact, and the branch lines which were to close in the late 1950s and early 1960s were still open. Hopefully this will give the reader a better idea of the railway in its entirety, and not in its present somewhat "truncated" state. Except where otherwise stated, the figures in brackets after the station name give the distance in miles and chains from Cairns and the height above sea level. In the case of branch lines, distances are from the junction station.)

Cairns (1,043m. 11c. from Brisbane; 10ft.) is the headquarters of the Cairns Division, and under the control of a District Superintendent who is stationed here. The present station, located in McLeod Street, was opened in August 1955 replacing an earlier structure which had dated in part to the opening of the railway, and houses the District administrative staff as well as providing suitable amenities for passengers. The present main line platform is 760'0" long, capable of handling the longest trains, and a bay platform on the north-eastern side is of sufficient length to handle trains bound for the Tablelands. Opposite the main platform is a smaller island platform which is reached by a footbridge from the main platform. The signalling at the time of our survey was somewhat primitive, being controlled from a small elevated lever frame, operating signals protecting conflicting routes at the south end of the yard. Opposite the island platform is the goods yard, and beyond the engine shed and locomotive, carriage and wagon workshops.

During the season, Cairns is one of Australia's most popular tourist centres and the tourists can enjoy such attractions as Green Island and its underwater observatory, Lake Placid, the Crystal Cascades, the Cook Highway to Mossman and Port Douglas, Fairyland, near Kuranda, the Atherton Tableland, the Palmerston Highway from Millaa Millaa to Innisfail, the Crater lakes and falls on the Tableland, and last but not least, the train trip from Cairns to Kuranda and the Barron Falls, one of the most spectacular rail journeys in Australia.

The Cairns Harbour Board's wharves for coastal and overseas shipping are served by a 74-chain branch line, which crosses Spence Street, and after passing the old Cairns-Mulgrave Tramway station and the Cairns goods shed and yard, curves around along the waterfront of Trinity Bay, passing various sidings serving the wharves and ends at the northern end of the wharf sheds. A second branch line turns out of Spence Street at Bunda Street, through the old Tramway station, and continues down Dutton Street serving various sidings and terminating at what is known as the Overseas Wharf.

The main line to Mareeba leaves Cairns station and proceeds in a north-westerly direction through the city and suburbs, paralleling Lily Creek. Just after the Upward Street level crossing, the present line deviates from the original formation which runs parallel to the main line, but across the creek, for a distance of about three quarters of a mile. There are various sidings along this section before *Aeroglen* (3m. 20c., 8ft.) is reached, serving Cairns Airport, and around the base of Lumley Hill to *Stratford* (4m. 55c.) and *Freshwater* (6m. 14c.). The line then passes over one of the 2'0" gauge tramways from the C.S.R.'s Hambledon Sugar Mill, and because of it's low height, two diesel locomotives at the mill are fitted with special collapsible cabs to work under the bridge. *Redlynch* (7m. 15c., 34ft.) is the bottom of the Cairns Range climb and is a staff station with a fork line for turning engines, the climb up the Range, commencing from the end of the fork line points. (There will be continuous reference made, in the narrative that follows, to various railway grades, i.e. 1 in 50 or 1 in 60. To explain, for every fifty or sixty feet of horizontal distance that the line travels, it rises vertically for a height of one foot over that distance.) For the first four miles, the line climbs at 1 in 50, with 5 chain radius curves. The line has now turned south, and the curves are easy to *Jungara* (8m. 47c., 169ft.), though half a mile beyond this station, the line turns through a 180 degree 5 chain radius curve to take it in a northerly direction along the side of the range. Just after this curve, the line enters the first tunnel of fifteen on the Range climb to Kuranda, and two miles beyond is the second tunnel, which is three-quarters of a mile in a direct line from Redlynch, but nearly four miles by rail. As the line continues to climb, there are now excellent views of the sugar cane lands towards Cairns. A number of tunnels are now encountered along with many small bridges, a succession of five chain curves, and some as sharp as four chains. For the next three miles, the line

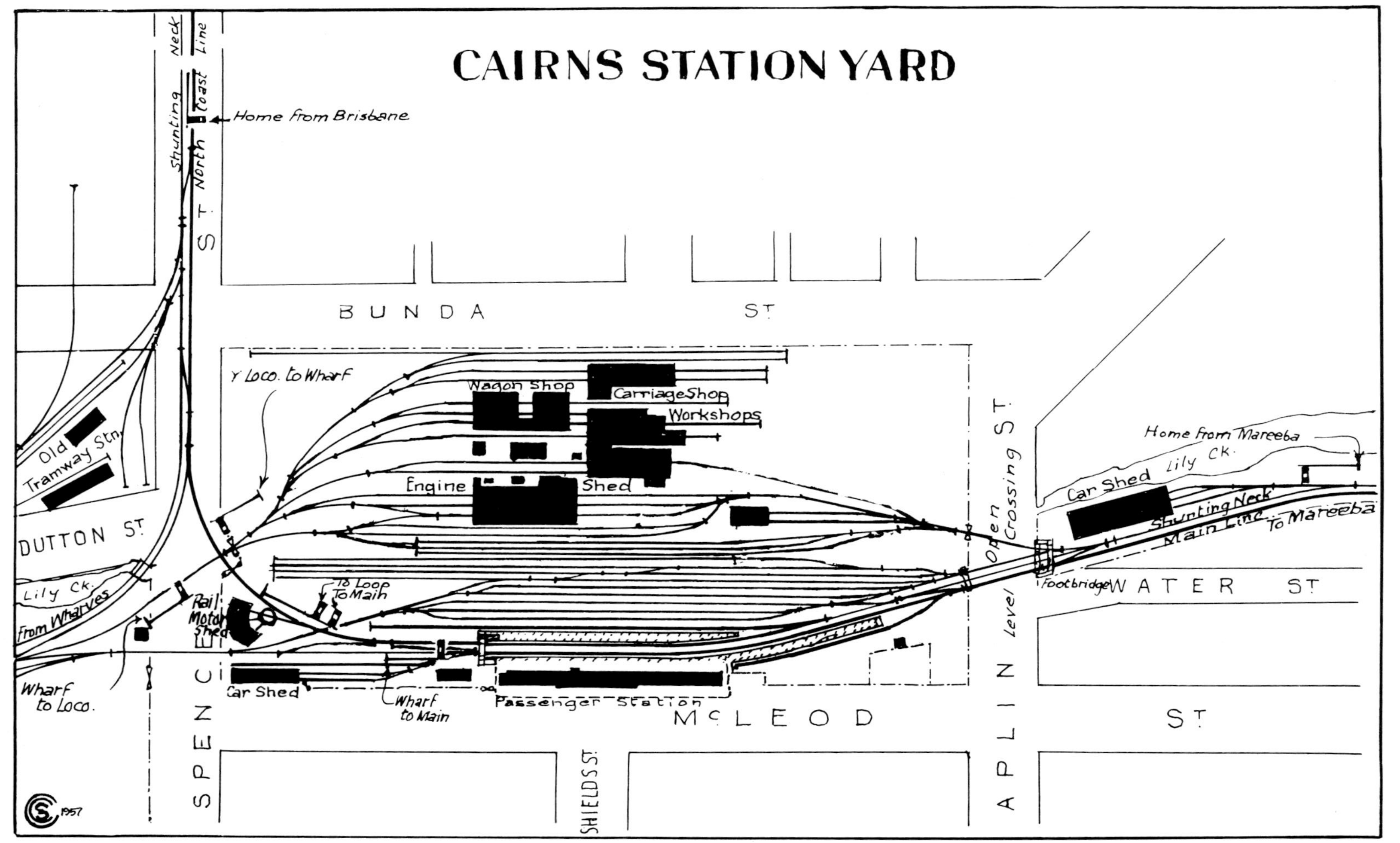

CAIRNS STATION YARD
Shunting Neck
North Coast Line
Home from Brisbane
ST
BUNDA ST
Old Tramway Stn
DUTTON ST
Lily Ck.
From Wharves
Wharf to Loco.
Y Loco. to Wharf
Wagon Shop
Carriage Shop
Workshops
Engine Shed
To Loop To Main
Rail Motor Shed
Car Shed
Wharf to Main
Passenger Station
SPENC
McLEOD ST
SHIELDS ST
APLIN
Open Level Crossing ST
Home from Mareeba
Lily Ck.
Car Shed
Shunting Neck
Main Line To Mareeba
Footbridge
WATER ST
1957

Above: Cairns Station in the 1880s with the two original Cairns Railway B13 class 4-6-0s. Nos. 1 and 2. built by Dubs in 1887 and 1886 respectively.

(Cairns Historical Society, courtesy E. Ward)

Below: The original Cairns Station building, 1922, a classic example of early colonial station architecture.

(Cairns Historical Society, courtesy E. Ward)

Above: Cairns station yard in 1908, a rare view showing the 0-6-0 crane tank engine No. 1. built by Beyer Peacock in 1902, performing the shunting duties.

(Cairns Historical Society, courtesy E. Ward)

Below: Chinese market gardeners unload their wares from a train at Cairns Station in the early 1900s.

(G. Bond Collection)

Unloading log timber at Cairns Wharf with an electric crane about 1925.
(J. Knowles Collection)

PB15 class No. 559 prepares to depart from Cairns with the "Tourist Train" for Kuranda in 1946.

(Late K.J.C. Rogers, courtesy G. Bond)

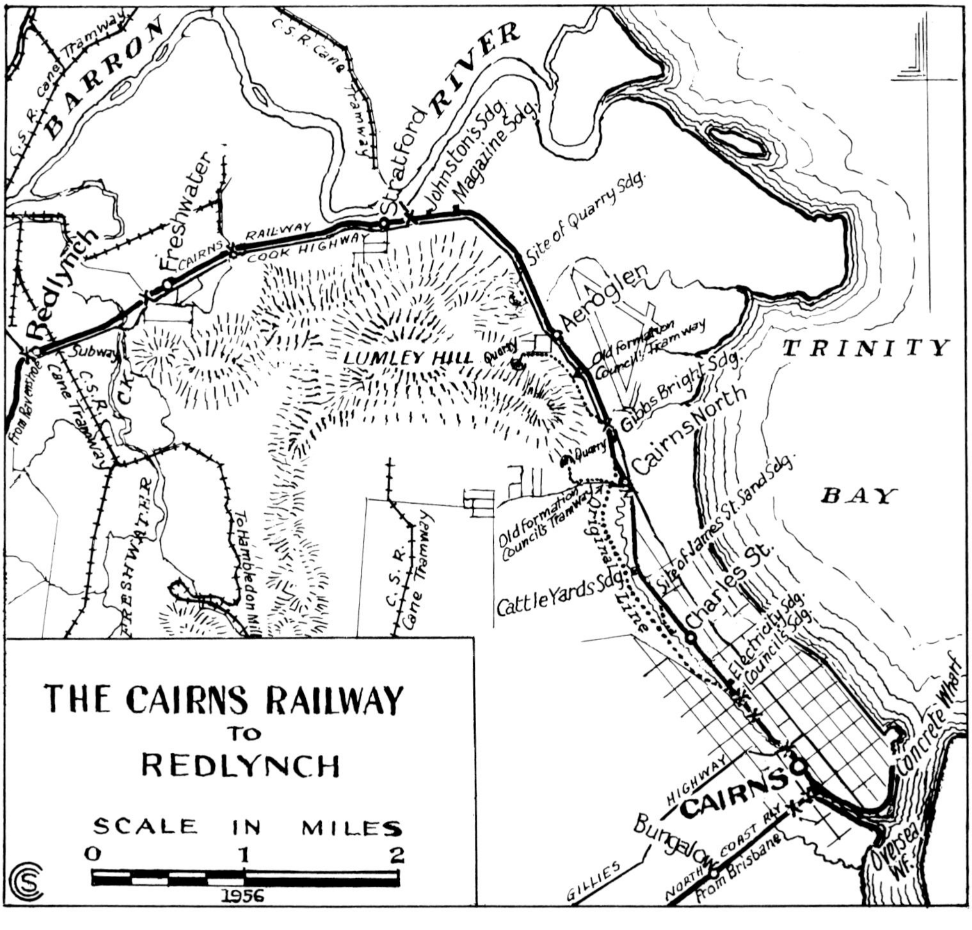

THE CAIRNS RAILWAY
TO
REDLYNCH

SCALE IN MILES
0 1 2
1956

passes around, North Peak Mountain, and about 11½ miles from Cairns, the grades ease to 1 in 55/60 for the rest of the ascent. There are no less than ten tunnels in this section, together with viaducts over steep ravines down the mountain side. Between tunnels nine and ten, the line is opposite the mouth of the Barron Gorge, but the track curves round to enter the Stoney Creek gorge, and below to the right can be seen Lake Placid.

Passing through tunnel 11, with its five chain reverse curves, and tunnel twelve, the line arrives at the entrance to tunnel thirteen. Just before the tunnel mouth are two signals, the home signal for Stoney Creek station, and below it on the same post, a "calling on" arm to advise trains to draw up to the loop points at the other end of the tunnel. There is also a starting signal for Down trains, this enabling the guard, after having locked the loop points at Stoney Creek, to give "right-away" to the engine crew to proceed down the Range. *Stoney Creek* (14m. 11c., 674ft.) is an unattended staff station, with watering facilities for engines, situated in a pleasant glade of tropical jungle, and the rail level platform is placed between the main line and the

Memorial to the Range Railway builders—Robbs Monument.

(R. Deskins)

loop. In the seven miles from Redlynch, the line has climbed 640 feet, and at the time of our survey (1956), ascending (up) passenger trains were allowed 30 minutes, and goods trains, 45 minutes, for the climb. In the descending (Down) direction, passenger trains were allowed 27 minutes and goods trains 37 minutes, the latter including time for a stop to recharge the air brake reservoirs, a very necessary part of railway operation on the Range.

Leaving Stoney Creek station, the line climbs into the head of the Stoney Creek gorge and a quarter of a mile beyond the station, curves around a 4 chain curve and across the famous Stoney Creek bridge below the Stoney Creek falls, the water from these falls, when rain is heavy, spraying onto the train. It must surely be one of the most photographed bridges in Australia!! The line now continues one and a half miles to the north-east, through tunnel fourteen, and around the steep sides of Red Bluff to enter the Barron Gorge. It is now no longer possible to see the sights of the cane fields stretching away to Cairns, and the passenger is confronted with the steep rocky and jungle-clad sides of the gorge. Half a mile after passing around the base of Red Bluff is the last tunnel on the Range climb, number fifteen, which has a 7½ chain curve at one end, a 15 chain curve at the other, and a 5 chain curve in the middle—it is also the longest of the fifteen tunnels.

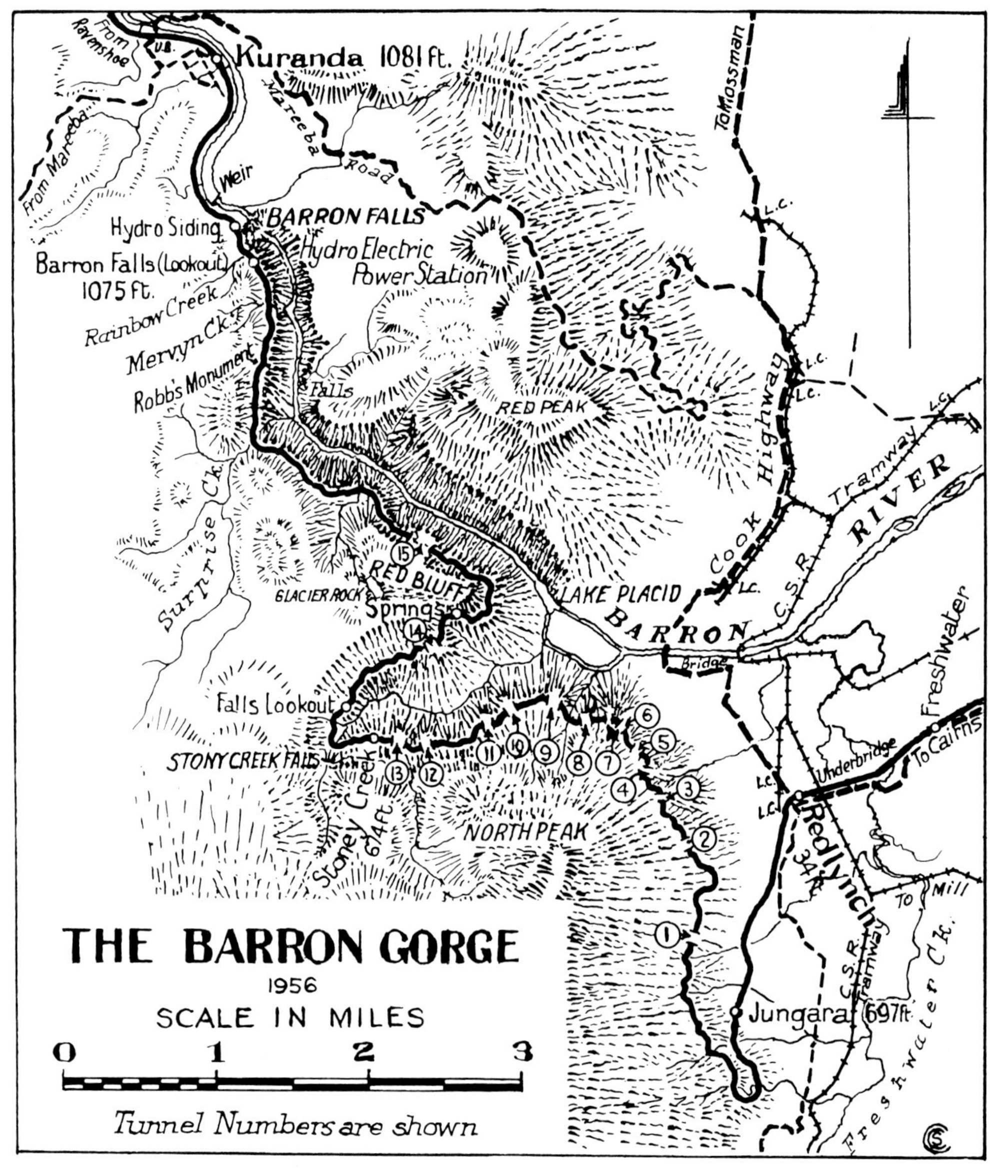

A superb view showing PB15 339 and the "Tourist Train" climbing the Range, and beyond the Barron River stretching away into the distance towards Cairns. The reason for the ornate livery applied to 339 is not known (note the stars on the front toolboxes, and the tender and cab lining) however it could have been in connection with the introduction of the "Grandstand Train" which would date the photo as after 1936.

(J.L. Buckland Collection)

The line continues climbing along the Barron River Gorge on a ledge cut into the cliff face, some 700 feet above the river and there are still a number of bridges over ravines in the mountain-side. About 18 miles from Cairns is Robb's Monument, a huge rock weighing over a ton, which is situated on the gorge side of the track, and remains from construction days as a memorial to John Robb and the men who built the Range railway. The climb ends at *Barron Falls* (19m. 5c., 1,075ft.) where there is a platform to view the falls of the same name. Normally the falls are only flowing heavily in the wet season, the construction of the Tinnaroo Dam further upstream having reduced the flow of water considerably. On occasions when tourists visit the area, the flood gates of the dam are opened to allow a reasonable flow of water over the falls. The main body of water is now diverted behind the falls to the hydro—electric power station situated in the gorge at the base of the falls, and the nearby *Hydro Siding* (19m. 29c., 1,075ft.) was provided to handle material and stores for the power station.

The line continues to climb slightly to *Kuranda* (20m. 52c., 1,081ft.), a staff station with raised platform, refreshment room for the convenience of passengers, and fully interlocked signal cabin, the only example of such equipment north of Townsville. Watering and turning facilities for engines are provided, the latter being accomplished by means of a 42 ft. diameter turntable instead of the more normal fork line, this being brought about by the station's cramped location. Kuranda station is well known throughout Australia for the fernery on and around the station, giving the whole area a most pleasing appearance. It is interesting to note that since the closing of the Cooktown Railway and the Rumula Branch, Kuranda is the most northerly station in Queensland. Before the 1500 class diesel electric locomotives took over from steam in 1959, the 120-130 ton loads of the PB15 and B15Con. classes were amalgamated here. Banking and double-heading of steam engines (and diesels for that matter) is not permitted on the range section due to the light bridges, however since diesels have taken over, loads have increased and Kuranda has lost most of its importance, though it still remains the terminus point for the Tourist Train from Cairns.

A B15 class 4-6-0 in original style with a mixed train for the Tableland heads upgrade through Stoney Creek Station about 1911. Note the star on the smokebox door.

(Cairns Historical Society, courtesy E. Ward)

Above: Railmotor RM 53 pauses briefly in the tropical splendour of Stoney Creek station before heading on for Kuranda with a Tourist Special in 1961.

(J. Knowles)

Below: Timber has always been an important traffic for the Cairns Railway and here a B13 class hauls a load of log timber downgrade towards Cairns near Barron Falls about 1910-11.

(A.R.H.S. Queensland Division Collection)

Increasing tourist traffic led to the reconstruction of Kuranda station, and these two views show the new station buildings, which also included a refreshment room, soon after it had been opened in 1915. The tower-shaped structure in the foreground of the lower photo is a lift for passenger's luggage.

(Queensland Railways)

Two B13 class engines on a Mixed train head past Barron Falls for Cairns. As double-heading has never been permitted on the Range, it is a little difficult to understand why two engines were being used.

(Queensland Railways)

REDLYNCH

From Cairns
HIGHWAY
2 levers
3 levers
Up Home
Up Distant
Gate
Gate
Level Crossing
Down Dist.
Down Outer Home
Down Home

STONEY CREEK

Guards Signal
Tunnel 13
Calling on Up Home
LOOP
MAIN
2 levers
Office
Lever
To Ravenshoe
Down Home

KURANDA

Goods Shed
GOODS SIDING
No. 1 PFM. RD.
PLATFORM
Water Column
No. 2 PLATFORM ROAD
LOOP
BACK ROAD
Turntable
Key from Cabin 'O'

YUNGABURRA

Up Home
Veneer Factory
Loading Shed
Overbridge
Pit
Tank
2 levers
Stock Race
Down Home
© 1953

MILLAA MILLAA

Engine Shed
Tank
Up Home
Goods Shed
Rail Motor Shed
Up Outer Home
Stock Races
2 levers
Station
Butter Factory

306

Above: The entrance to Kuranda Station yard from Cairns—the Down Inner Home bracket, a typical Queensland Railways McKenzie & Holland style signal, 1962.

(E. Ward)

Centre Page Spread: This scene probably best typifies the Cairns Range Railway—the curved steel bridge, the water fall, and the lush green undergrowth. B15 Con. class 4-6-0 No. 306 is seen crossing Stoney Creek Falls bridge with an A.R.H.S. Queensland Division special train in 1965.

Below: Railmotor RM 79, originally used on the Etheridge Railway to Forsayth, on a morning run to Mareeba in 1961. Note the sand boxes, screw coupling, and buffer plate, relics of its Forsayth days.

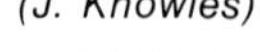
(J. Knowles)

Above: The attractive signal cabin and 37-lever frame at Kuranda in 1961. The signalling arrangements here are fully interlocked, the only such example of this equipment north of Townsville.

(E. Ward)

Below: PB15 class No. 547 is turned on the turntable at Kuranda after working a "Tourist Train" from Cairns in 1964. Built by Cowans Sheldon, Carlisle, England, in 1884, the table is provided due to the cramped location not allowing the more normal fork line.

(E. Ward)

An Up (to Cairns) railmotor, RM 93, crosses a Down (to Mareeba) goods train at Kuranda station in the 1950s. *(Late K.J.C. Rogers Collection, courtesy G. Bond)*

To give the reader a complete picture of the Cairns Railway, it is necessary to give a brief description of the other lines in the area.

KURANDA—MAREEBA—HERBERTON—RAVENSHOE.

After leaving Kuranda, the line continues to follow the Barron River, travelling through jungle country for the next 10 miles, but grades in this section are only 1 in 70 and there are fewer curves, though many of them are still sharp. At *Fairyland* (22m. 7c., 1,111ft.), a scenic walk into the jungle begins, and the line continues through other small stations to the Surprise Creek bridge, the lightness of this structure being one of the reasons why double-heading is not permitted. *Koah* (31m.32c., 1,192ft.) is the first staff station and three miles further on the line swings away from the Barron River, but crosses it at Pukanja. *Biboobra* (46m.21c. 1,327ft.) is the next staff station, with watering facilities and fork line for turning engines; it was also junction for the Mt. Molloy-Rumula Branch. The line continues to climb to *Mareeba* (46m.21c., 1,327ft.) a staff station with watering and turning facilities for engines, and is the largest town in the area. It is a large cattle selling centre for the Cape York Peninsula area, and also for the tobacco growing areas west of the town. It is not actually on the Atherton Tableland, but is situated some 1,100 feet below it and for this reason is somewhat drier. The line to Mareeba was opened in 1893, but is was not until 1910 that it was extended to Herberton. After leaving Mareeba, the line climbs up to the Atherton Tableland through open country, and then on to the Evelyn Tableland by way of the steep grades of the Herberton Range.

The Atherton Tableland is very fertile and the original jungle areas have been cleared for dairying, maize and other crops. The Evelyn Tableland is now mostly devoted to timber-getting. Between Mareeba and Tolga, the line crosses over irrigation canals carrying water from the Tinaroo Dam, 10 miles east of Atherton and completed in 1958, to the land in the Dimbulah area in the west. Grades south of Mareeba are 1 in 50 to Tolga, 1 in 70 to Wongabel, 1 in 33 over the Herberton Range to Moomin, 1 in 60 (northbound) to Herberton, 1 in 66 (both directions) to Wondecla, and 1 in 50 (both directions) to Ravenshoe, giving some idea of the difficult country traversed. Until 1959, this section was worked mainly by PB15 and B15Con.locos after the disappearance of the earlier classes, and their loads on the Herberton Range were restricted to 90 and 100 tons respectively. It was for this reason that a C17 class, based on Mareeba, was brought up from Cairns, increasing the train loading to 150 tons. At *Rocky Creek* (59m.77c., 2,154ft.), two water tanks were provided for engine purposes as double-headed trains were allowed to work through from Mareeba to Atherton, but not beyond there on the Herberton Range. *Tolga* (64m.23c., 2,460ft.) is a staff station with watering and turning facilities for engines, and was junction for the branch line to Millaa Millaa. It is also the centre of a large maize growing area, and silos are provided for storage of this commodity. The line continues to *Atherton* (67m.41c., 2,469ft) and centre of the rich and scenic Atherton Tableland. The line drops down to *Wongabel* (71m.53c., 2,471ft.) before commencing to climb up the Herberton Range, with a maximum grade of 1 in 33, there being a stop to recharge air reservoirs at 73m.54c., and at Carrington Falls, a water tank for engine purposes on a piece of easier grade, all being located in this section. Just before the summit, there is a tunnel at 76m.69c., situated on a steep grade of 1 in 36½.

The line now reaches *Herberton* (81m. 59c., 2,893ft.), once an important tin mining centre, but now only a shadow of its former self, and rich in historic interest. Tin was first discovered here in 1879 on the nearby Wild River, and the rough country between here and Irvinebank, and west at Mt. Garnet, is also rich in tin, however by the time the railway reached Herberton, the tin mining was beginning to decline. The town is now supported mainly by secondary boarding schools. After leaving Herberton, the line drops down slightly before continuing its climb up to *Tumoulin* (98m.72c., 3,165ft.), the highest station in Queensland, being 130ft. higher than The Summit on the Southern Line to Wallangarra, and 109ft. higher than Bapaume on the now closed Amiens Branch from Cotton Vale, also on the Southern Line. The line continues another four miles to *Ravenshoe* (103m.32c., 2,969ft.), which, like Herberton, has watering and turning facilities for engines, is a staff station, and terminus of the main line from Cairns, the section from Herberton being opened in 1916. The town is an important timber centre.

MT. MOLLOY—RUMULA BRANCH.

This 26 mile long line left the main line to Mareeba at Biboobra, the first 19 miles to *Mt. Molloy* (19m.29c., 1,308ft.) being built by the Mt. Molloy Co. to serve its copper mine and smelter there which had commenced operations in 1902. In 1926 the line was extended to *Rumula* (27m.8c., 1,358ft.), the new line leaving the old station on a spur line and a new station had to be built on the extension. Rumula was an unattended staff station, with turning facilities for engines. Grades were 1 in 45 to Rumula and 1 in 40 in the opposite direction. The line was closed in 1964.

MILLAA MILLAA BRANCH.

Leaving the main line to Herberton at Tolga, this 36 mile branch line served the most populated area of the Atherton Tableland, and was therefore very busy. The first section to *Yungaburra* (10m.23c., 2,185ft.), the first staff station, was opened in 1910. The line was extended to *Kureen* (17m.39c., 2,429ft.) and on to *Malanda* (18m.77c., 2,405ft.), the second staff

Picnic day was an important event in the Railway calender in the early days. Here a group of "dignitaries" pose for their photo with a B13 class which hauled the Railway Employees Picnic Train from Cairns to Biboohra in 1907. *(W. Tierney.)*

Above: Mareeba station yard with B15 Con. class No. 42 (an ex-Chillagoe Co. engine) on an Up Mixed train off the Chillagoe line in 1964.

(B.J. Webber)

Below: Railmotor RM 75 stands under the overall arched roof shed at Mareeba station in 1967.

(B. Webber)

Above: B15 Con. class No. 315 shunting at Herberton station in the 1920s.

(W.D. Warren, courtesy G. Bond)

Below: A B13 class at Kulara on the Millaa Millaa branch about 1914.

(A.R.H.S. Queensland Division Collection)

station with an engine triangle, later in the same year. Malanda is the centre of an important dairying area, and a large butter factory is located here. The section from Malanda to *Jaggan* (23m.43c., 2,493ft.) was opened in 1915, and the next section on to *Tarzali* (27m.13c., 2,470ft.,) also with an engine triangle, and an unattended staff station, was completed in 1916. It was another five years before the line was opened throughout to *Millaa Millaa* (36m.41c., 2,692ft), terminus of the line, which was a staff station and had engine watering and turning facilities, as well as a small engine shed and railmotor shed. The branch line passed through very hilly country and to avoid steep grades, followed an extremely winding course. The main produce of the area served was dairy products and timber. The line was closed throughout in 1964.

CHILLAGOE CO. MAIN LINE—MAREEBA TO MUNGANA.

The Chillagoe Railway & Mines Ltd. built and operated one of the largest privately owned railways in Australia, a total of 307 track miles being built between 1899 and 1915. The company was first formed in 1893, and one of its directors was John Moffat, well known for his pioneering work in the mining industry of North Queensland, The company tried unsuccessfully to interest the Queensland Government in building a railway to serve its mining interests in the Chillagoe and Etheridge areas. After reforming the company in 1899 to provide the necessary finance, the Chillagoe Co. set about building the line itself, with full Government approval. The company's career was destined, however, like so many of its counterparts, to be a short one and after the North Queensland mining "boom" had reached its peak about 1908, it began to decline rapidly, and just after the First World War, the Government took over the whole operation, the most viable part probably being the railway.

The main line leaves the Cairns-Ravenshoe line at Mareeba and immediately commences to climb the Great Dividing Range, the next 7 miles being on grades of 1 in 55. The line then crosses about thirty miles of agricultural country, now devoted mainly to tobacco grow-

C17 class 4-8-0 No. 250 climbs away from Herberton with a mixed train for Mareeba in July 1966.
(R. Deskins)

ing, to reach *Dimbulah* (26m.75c. 1,515ft.), the first staff station, with engine watering and turning facilities, and junction for the branch line to Mt. Mulligan. *Boonmoo* (35m.14c., 1,616ft.) was once an important station with an engine triangle, being transhipment point for the 2'0" gauge Stannary Hills & Irvinebank Tramway operated between 1902 and 1936. This line ran for some 30 miles into the rugged country to the southeast to serve tin and copper mines and smelters. If it still existed today, its main line through the Eureka Creek gorge would prove equally as interesting as the climb up the Cairns Range. Some forty miles from Mareeba, the line commences to climb the Featherbed Range, with 1 in 50 grades, to *Lappa Junction* (55m.64c., 1,956ft.), a staff station with engine triangle, and junction for the Mt. Garnet branch line. This station was also the end of the first construction section, the line being opened to here in 1900. The line then drops down to *Almaden* (74m. 48c., 1,619ft.), another staff station, with watering and turning facilities for engines, and as junction for the Chillagoe and Forsayth lines, an important station from the operational point of view. In steam days, engines of stock trains to Mt. Surprise were recoaled here, crews changed, and a small engine shed was later provided to house one of the diesel mechanical locomotives. Today it has lost a lot of its importance, but still remains a control point for the Chillagoe Co. lines.

After leaving Almaden, the main line turns away to follow a north-easterly course and enters what used to be an important mining field which stretched for some 15 to 20 miles. *Chillagoe* (92m.20c., 1,156ft.), a staff station with triangle, was once the largest town west of Cairns, but now is virtually a "ghost" town. Nearby are the famous limestone Chillagoe Caves, a popular tourist attraction. Grades in the section from Almaden to Chillagoe are 1 in 50 in the Up direction, and 1 in 45 in the Down direction. About half a mile beyond Chillagoe is the site of the *Chillagoe Smelters* (92m.69c., 1,148ft.) which were headquarters for the Chillagoe Co. in the days of private ownership, and the company's locomotive shed was also situated here along with workshop facilities. The smelters were first "blown in" in 1901 and continued in use, sometimes intermittently, until 1943 when they were closed down completely. The smelter chimneys, the most substantial remains, still dominate the surrounding countryside as silent reminders of a once affluent era at the turn of the century. In the surrounding area are the remnants of many famous mining concerns which have a fascinating, if complicated, history—today, regretably, little remains, and the area depends on the cattle industry. The continuation of the main line from Chillagoe which was completed throughout in 1901, has always been treated more as a branch line, the remaining ten miles through mining country to *Mungana* (102m.70c., 1,123ft.) being kept open mainly to serve to cattle industry, large yards being provided on the engine triangle for loading purposes. Substantial numbers of cattle are trucked here in the season for railing to the meatworks in the south. The 1 in 40 grades in the Down direction (1 in 45 in the Up direction) often make it necessary for these cattle trains to work in two sections up to a dividing siding about midway to Chillagoe.

THE ETHEREDGE BRANCH.

This line to Forsayth leaves the main line at Almaden and proceeds in a south-westerly direction across most uninteresting country. Once again the Queensland Government agreed to the Chillagoe Co. constructing the line, but wished to retain ownership on completion and an unusual working arrangement existed whereby the Government hired Chillagoe Co. trains to work the line for the Chillagoe Co.!!! The line was completed for its 142 mile length in 1911. Construction of the line was of the cheapest possible means resulting in steep grades, many of them 1 in 40, and sharp "momentum" grades on river crossings. The end of the first staff section is at *Ootann* (7m.71c., 1,460ft) which, following cyclone damage to the line in 1927, was the extent of steam operation till 1950 when this was extended to *Mt. Surprise*, (66m.78c., 1,492ft.), a staff station with engine watering and turning facilities. Steam engines never worked further south than Mt. Surprise after 1927, the line being worked entirely by railmotors until the first diesel mechanical locomitive, built specially for this line, arrived in 1939, this type later being increased to four and taking over all operations until complete dieselisation in 1968. *Einasleigh* (101m. 3c., 1,483ft.), a staff station with engine turning facilities, was the site of a copper mine owned by the Chillagoe Co., and one of the main reasons for building the line. After the mine closed in 1922, the surrounding area has been devoted mostly to cattle. The country traversed so far is generally undulating, but about ten miles from Einasleigh, the line climbs up and over the Newcastle Range and plateau, before dropping down the Delaney Creek gorge using steep grades and curves (some as sharp as 4 chain radius) to *Forsayth* (142m.25c., 1,329ft.), terminus of the line, a staff station, and with watering and turning facilities for engines. Even though steam engines have not worked here since 1927, the water tower is still retained in use for the permanent way gangs. Forsayth was on the edge of an important mining area which centred around Georgetown further to the south-west, but for some reason, although plans for extension were mooted, the line remained

Chillagoe Railway & Mining Co.'s B15 class No. 5 heads a work train onto the Etheridge Railway (Forsayth branch) at Almaden during the construction period about 1907-08.

(G. Bond Collection)

where it was and was never continued. There were however, two mine sidings which ran for a couple of miles to serve nearby mines but these were dismantled when the mining ceased in the early years of the century.

MT. GARNET BRANCH.

Wilcox & Everend were contractors for this line which was opened in 1901-02 and built primarily at the instigation of the Mt. Garnet Freehold Copper & Silver Co., who later sold their interests to the Government in 1914. Latterly the area has gained importance for its tin mining. The branch left the Chillagoe Co. main line at Lappa Junction, and after curving around the western side of the Featherbed Range, dropped down to cross undulating country to *Ord* (16m.3c., 1,996ft.). The line then begins a second climb, this time over the Great Dividing Range, before running down to the terminus of the line, *Mt. Garnet* (32m.55c., 2,136ft.), end of the only staff section, with turning facilities for engines. Watering facilities were provided en route. Mt. Garnet was later served by the Northern Inland Highway and it is surprising that the line remained open as long as it did—it was closed in 1963. The ruling grade on the branch was 1 in 40 and curves were as sharp as 4 chain radius.

MT. MULLIGAN BRANCH.

The mining fraternity must have viewed with some interest the discovery of coal at Mt. Mulligan as they no doubt thought that their fuel problems were over. A mine was established and in 1915 a branch line was built to serve it. The line branched from the main line at Dimbulah and ran over undulating country with grades of 1 in 30 in the Up direction and 1 in 40 in the Down direction. The main intermediate station was at *Thornborough* (17m.28c.,) a little over half way to *Mt. Mulligan* (29m.64c.) with watering and turning facilities for engines, and end of the single staff section. To turn the engines, a 40ft. diameter turntable was provided, the only one located on the ex-Chillagoe Co. lines, the more normal method used being a triangle or fork line. The mine opened in 1915, but from the very beginning was below expectations, though the coal was in sufficient quantity to cater for the needs of the Railway Dept., Irvinebank Co., Chillagoe Co. and Cairns Harbour Board, as well as domestic use. In 1921 the mine was the site of a most disastrous coal gas explosion, claiming a number of lives, and resulting in a Royal Commission into safety procedure. Mining did re-commence, but by the mid-1950s, the coal reserves began to diminish and the mine closed down in 1957. With the reason for its ex-

Above: Stannary Hills & Irvinebank Tramway 2'0" guage 0-6-2 tank engine No. 3 built by Avonside in 1908, crossing Gibbs Creek bridge at Irvinebank about 1914.

(G. Bond Collection)

Below: A busy scene at Stannary Hills station about 1910 on the 2'0" gauge Stannary Hills and Irvinebank Tramway.

(L. Cuffe Collection)

istance disappeared, the railway was closed in 1958.

It seems that discussions with the Chillagoe Co. with a view to Governmet purchase due to financial difficulties, were first made in the early years of the First World War, but the war delayed progress. In 1918 the Government made a full valuation and purchase was effected, the hand-over taking place on 20th June 1919. The railway was absorbed into the Queensland Railways, and the mining interests came under the control of the State Mines Dept. The Chillagoe Co. owned its own locomitives and rolling stock, and these are discussed briefly in the relative sections at the end of this booklet.

CAIRNS—MULGRAVE TRAMWAY AND THE NORTH COAST LINE.

In 1895 the Mulgrave Central Milling Co. was formed and set up a sugar mill at Nelson (now Gordonvale). To serve the mill, the Cairns Divisional Board arranged for a Government loan to construct a 3'6" guage tramway from Cairns and the line was completed in 1897. The terminus of the line was located near the intersection of Spence and Bunda Streets, and although separate from, connection was made with the Government railway via a short line to the Queensland Railways wharf extension. The Aloomba Estate was developed as a cane plantation to supply the Hambledon Mill further south, and the Cairns Divisional Board therefore extended its tramway a further four miles in 1898 from Gordonvale to Aloomba, the cane being railed north, later direct to the Hambledon Mill on a short branch line built in 1905. The Board was re-constituted as the Cairns Shire Council in 1902, and when it was anticipated that a further sugar mill, the Babinda Mill, would be built, the Shire extended its line further south, 13 miles to Harvey's Creek, opened in 1903, and on to Babinda in 1910, giving a total distance of 37m. 25c. from Cairns.

Anticipating the pending completion of the North Coast Railway from Brisbane to Cairns the Queensland Railways purchased the Shire Tramway in 1911, and the locomotives and rolling stock which the Shire owned (including some engines purchased from the Q.R.) were incorporated into the then-isolated Cairns Railway stock. Queensland Railways extended the line from Babinda south to Pawngilly in 1912 and onwards to Daradgee in 1919 which took the line to end of the Cairns Railway District's southern boundary. Here southward construction halted awaiting connection with the construction proceeding from the south, though it was to be another twelve years before the final link was made. By the end of 1924, completion of the Daradgee Bridge was approaching and on 31st. October 1924, the final span was rolled into position. On 8th. December 1924, a bedecked B13 class 4-6-0 from Cairns hauled the first official train over the bridge and the 1,043 mile long line from Brisbane to Cairns was finally complete. The Cairns Railway's isolation ceased to exist after thirty-seven years of being one of the Queensland Railway's northern outposts.

Cairns-Mulgrave Tramway ex-Queensland Railways B12 class 2-6-0 on a mixed train at the Cairns tramway station some time after 1903. Note the "toastrack" style tramway carriages.

(G. Bond Collection)

Above: Cairns-Mulgrave Tramway 4-6-0 No. 5 (later Q.R. B13 class), specially built for the Tramway by Baldwin in 1908, on a mixed train consisting predominantly of sugar cane, at Aloomba.

(J.L. Buckland Collection)

Below: The driver of PB15 class No. 744 enjoys a quick "cuppa" at Innisfail about 1929 before heading north with the Townsville-Cairns Mail train. Note the stars on the front of highly polished engine.

(C. Henshaw)

Above: Cairns engine shed and coal stage, 1966. The engines are, left to right, a PB15 class 4-6-0, PB15 class No. 597, C17 class 4-8-0 No. 817 and a B15 Con. class 4-6-0.

(E. Ward)

Below: B15 Con. class 4-6-0 No. 298 near Mareeba about 1930. This engine was built by the Yorkshire Engine Co. in 1895 as a B15 and was converted to the style seen here in 1913.

(A.R.H.S. Queensland Division Collection)

Steam Locomotives Of The Cairns Railway.

Cairns locomotive shed in steam days was always one of the more interesting sheds in Queensland because it always had to rely on the smaller types of engines for the light bridges on the Range section. Three types of locomotives, the B13 class 4-6-0, B15 class 4-6-0 (and its variant the B15 Converted) and the PB15 class 4-6-0 held almost undisputed sway for the seventy odd years that steam locomotives (solely) were in use in Cairns. It was not until the mid-1930s that any of the "larger" type of steam engines were stationed at Cairns, and then it was only a C16 class 4-8-0, which had by that time begun to be relegated to secondary duties, although they still were a very useful engine. A table showing the steam locomotives allocated to Cairns is appended elsewhere and covers the period from 1887 to 1960, the year in which the first main line diesel electric locomotive, a 1500 class, was stationed there. Diesels had of course worked into Cairns for many years prior to this, and the diesel mechanical 2-6-0 type had been in use on the Forsayth branch from before the Second World War.

Cairns had a sub-shed at Mareeba which covered most of the workings to the south and west of Mareeba. Locomotives were also stabled overnight at Ravenshoe and Millaa Millaa at various times to suit operating timetables. The Chillagoe Co. lines were originally served from the main Chillagoe Co. shed at Chillagoe smelters, about half a mile west of Chillagoe, but after the QR took these lines over in 1919, the operating was based on Mareeba. Overnight stabling was done at Mt. Mulligan, Mt. Garnet, Einasleigh and Forsayth, and occasionally at Almaden.When the DLs appeared they were based on Forsayth and Almaden, with engines being shedded variously at each end of the line. Since dieselisation however, all locomotives have been shedded at Cairns, working right through to their destination and stabling overnight when and where necessary.

The smallest engine to be shedded at Cairns was the D11½ class 0-6-0 crane tank built by Beyer Peacock in 1902, one of two intended for workshops use. Neither appear to have been successful in this capacity and both had their cranes removed in 1912. No. 1 was transferred to Cairns in 1907-08 for use at the workshops there, but was probably relegated to shunting duties after its crane was removed. It disappears from the records for Cairns in 1916-17, and as it was not officially scrapped until 1927 must have lain derelict for the intervening ten years. It is probable that this engine was the one almost sold to the Chillagoe State Smelters in 1924, but the sale was never completed.

The first B11 class 2-6-0 to come to Cairns was a small typically American style locomotive built by Baldwin in 1879, which arrived in 1888 from the Great Northern Railway at Townsville. It was hired to John Robb in the same year for use on the construction of the second section of the Range railway, and shared these duties with a similar engine named "Pioneer" which Robb was also using. There seems to have been free interchange of these two engines between contractor and Railway Dept. during the construction. The B11 lay idle at times between 1894 and 1896, and in 1897 was sold to the Cairns—Mulgrave Tramway where it worked until 1911 when it again returned to the QR. Its subsequent movements are a little doubtful, but it was scrapped in 1913.

"Pioneer", Robb's 2-6-0, was also built by Baldwin in 1879, reputedly for the contractors, J. & A. Overend. It saw extensive use throughout the State on various construction projects, including Robb's contract on the second section of the Range railway and McKenzie & Sutherland's Cairns-Herberton Railway contract. It was sold about 1898 to the Chillagoe Railway, becoming their first engine, and again worked on construction duties. It was out of service from 1900 to 1902, and from 1913 to 1923, during which time it was taken over by the QR in 1919. Although originally considered unfit for further services, it was overhauled and placed in use at Cairns as a B14 class in 1923, but only lasted a few years, being scrapped in 1927.

The B12 class 2-6-0s were a small type of engine of which the first were built by Kitson & Co. in 1869. The three engines that worked at Cairns were all taken over from the Cairns-Mulgrave Tramway in 1911, thus being reacquired by the QR who had sold all three to the tramway originally. They pottered around on light duties until the end of the First World War when two of them were withdrawn and lay idle until the late 1920s when they were scrapped, however the third, probably the best of the three, carried on until 1927.

The first two engines to work on the Cairns Railway were of the B13 class 4-6-0 built by Dubs in 1886 and 1887 and landed from the "Duke of Sutherland" and "Durunda" respectively, in 1887. These two engines, with the assistance of the small B11, were the sole motive power on the railway until 1894, having the honour of hauling the first train up the range section in 1891. Three other members of the class were eventually added to the fleet, and in 1908, one of them was hired to the Cairns—Mulgrave Tramway. In 1911 when the QR took over the tramway, it acquired a further B13, but

PB15 class No. 577 heads a goods train onto the main line after taking water at Gordonvale in 1952. *(G. Bond Collection)*

this one was unusual in that it had been built by Baldwin in 1908 as distinct from the other members of the class at Cairns which had been built in Britain. A total of nine B13s eventually worked at Cairns, including one from the isolated Cooktown Railway, this number being achieved in 1924-25. A B13 also had the distinction of hauling the first southbound train over the newly completed North Coast Line in 1924, and because the original Cairns—Mulgrave Tramway was available to no heavier engine, the B13s worked the through train service from Innisfail to Cairns until 1926 when the line was sufficiently strengthened to take PB15s. This led to their declining use and by 1928-30 only two remained, the last going in 1938-39, thus ending a fifty year association with the Cairns Railway. Some of the engines were also used during the construction of the Mt. Garnet line when they were hired to the contractors, Wilcox & Overend.

In 1901-02, the first of the "big" (for Cairns!!) engines arrived, two B15 class 4-6-0s. These engines had proved themselves to be very efficient and in the early years of the century, until the PB15 class began to appear in numbers, were responsible for most of the major passenger and goods services throughout the State, although their small driving wheels made them somewhat unsuitable for the fast schedules required by the mail trains. This led to the decision in 1903 to fit one of the class with larger driving wheels, and it was found that this solved the problem with regard to passenger train working, and they attained the name "Passenger B15s" or B15 Converteds, sometimes abbreviated to CB15. Eventually the majority of the class was so converted, including all the Cairns engines, and the class designation was finally settled as B15 Converted or B15 Con. From 1921 Cairns had no less than ten of these engines, and in the 1930s and 1940s, there were close to thirty for most of the time, and in the latter days of steam, Cairns had become a stronghold for some of the remaining examples, including No. 299, the first engine built by Walkers, and now set aside for preservation in Maryborough. The Chillagoe Co. wisely adopted the B15 type as its standard engine, and no less than seven were built for them between 1899 and 1909. One of them, however, never reached its destination, being taken over by the QR in 1909 during delivery, most likely because the Chillagoe Co. couldn't afford to pay for it!! The other six engines were all taken over by the QR in 1919 in company with the rest of the Chillagoe Co. locomotives stock. The class as a whole was extremely long lived, the last of them, No. 290, built by the Yorkshire Engine Co. in 1895, not being withdrawn until 1968, one year before the end of steam, and this engine is now preserve in the Steam Locomotive Museum at Redbank.

The next class of engine in size to be stationed at Cairns was the ubiquitous PB15 class 4-6-0.

First introduced in 1899 with Stephenson valve gear, and followed by a Walschaerts valve gear version in 1925, these engines became well known throughout the State, and took over most of the duties previously handled by the B13s and B15s. Although they had to be fired properly to get the best out of them, they were an extremely well liked and useful engine and with the disappearance of the older classes, were the only type of engine that could work anywhere in the state. Cairns mainly had the Stephenson valve gear version, although the Walschaerts type did work there at times. The PB15s did not come to Cairns until 1926 when the newly completed North Coast Line north of Innisfail had been sufficiently strengthened to take an engine heavier than a B13. Following the introduction of the "Sunshine Express" in 1935, although the C17 class 4-8-0s could work through to Babinda, the PBs were the only type allowed past there, so they took over at Innisfail, being rated to haul 285 tons over the final leg of the journey from Brisbane to Cairns. They continued on this duty until 1936 when the line had been further strengthened to allow the use of C17s all the way to Cairns. It was this class, with the B15Cons., which formed the bulk of the engines stationed at Cairns from the 1930s.

In 1935, the first of the C16 class 4-8-0s was stationed at Cairns. This class had been introduced in 1903, the class leader being the first locomotive to be built at the Railway Workshops at Ipswich. Although they were used early in their careers for handling passenger trains, their main purpose was the haulage of stock trains in northern and central Queensland. In later years they were used mainly on goods and shunting trains. During the Second World War, eleven of the class were transferred to the Central Australia Railway to assist in the war effort, but all had to be returned to Queensland when the motive power situation in Queensland worsened in the latter stages of the war. The C16s larger brothers, the C17 class, did not appear permanently in Cairns until after the Second World War. They had been introduced in 1920 and were, like the PB15s, later to be found in many parts of the State. A modified version of the original design was introduced in 1938, and later members of the second group, because of their unusual (for Queensland) brown livery soon gained them the nickname "Brown Bombers". The engines were well liked, easy to operate, and could be found on just about every duty imagineable, from air-conditioned trains to humble shunting duties. They were responsible

PB15 class 4-6-0 No. 596 on a Mareeba bound goods train at Kuranda in 1947.
(J.M. McMillan, J. Buckland Collection)

for the working of the "Sunshine Express" from 1936 until the early 1950s when the BB18¼ class 4-6-2s first appeared. On the Atherton Tableland, the Mareeba to Ravenshoe section was capable of carrying a C17, but the light bridges on the range section precluded them from working to Mareeba. However in 1959, it was decided to send one to Mareeba, from whence it would be possible to increase train loads from those handled by the PB15s. To achieve this, it was necessary to completely empty both engine (of boiler water) and tender (of coal and water) and then tow it to Mareeba where it could be refilled. The engine then remained there until it was required to go into 'shops or be transferred elsewhere, when the whole procedure would be repeated. No doubt it justified all the trouble taken!!

The last two engines to be dealt with that were stationed at Cairns were of a type which were unique to the North of Queensland, although well known in other States of Australia. These engines were of the Beyer Peacock "colonial" type 2-6-0, five examples of which were owned by the Chillagoe Co. They were all purchased about 1907, three of them second-hand from Western Australia, and two, possibly new, from Martin in South Australia. The two Martin engines were taken over in 1919 and were given the unusual class codings of AY and BY, the first letters being relics of their Chillagoe Co. days and the second letter "Y" probably originating from the fact that the type were known as the Y class in South Australia, where they were extensively used. They were the only class codes used in Queensland (apart from the Garratts) which did not give any indication of wheel arrangement and cylinder diameter.

Passing reference has been made to the diesel locomotive in this narrative, however it is not intended to describe these individually as their history is still being made and will therefore be a more appropriate part of the second century of the railway's history.

No, the B15 Con. class 4-6-0 is not about to work the "Sunlander"!! Ex-Chillagoe Co. No. 95 is seen shunting the empty carriages at Cairns.

(J. Armstrong)

Above: Mulgrave Central Sugar Mill's 0-6-0 tank engine "Pyramid", built by Hudswell Clarke in 1924, hauls a full load of sugar cane on the 2'0" gauge to the mill at Gordonvale. This engine is now preserved at Mareeba.
(Queensland Railways)

Below: Hambledon Sugar Mill's 2'0" guage 0-6-0 tender engine No. 5, also built by Hudswell Clarke in 1924, has its motion oiled near Redlynch before heading the mill with a load of sugar cane. Note the highly polished brass dome.
(J. Hayward, courtesy G. Bond)

Above: B15 Con. class No. 303 poses with the newly built carriages for the Townsville-Cairns Mail Train about 1925.
(Queensland Railways)

Below: This quaint old carriage, composite 1st. and 2nd class lavatory No. 187, built in 1889, complete with clerestory roof, was typical of the passenger stock to be found on the Cairns Railway prior to 1924.
(Late K.J.C. Rogers, courtesy G. Bond)

Cairns Railway Rolling Stock.

To describe the rolling stock used on the Cairns Railway in detail would require a medium sized volume, and it is therefore only possible to give brief details of the more interesting aspects of this important part of a railway's equipment. The accompanying tables show the various types of passenger carriages and goods wagons and the number in service from the beginnings of the Cairns Railway up to mid-1924. From this time, rolling stock returns included details of stock for the whole Q.G.R. system, and not as individual railways as had been the case prior to this. The change was of course brought about by the opening throughout of the North Coast Line from Brisbane to Cairns thus allowing free interchange of stock between the previously isolated systems. It is also important to mention here that prior to 1889 all these various railways had their own individual numbering systems, but in that year, all locomotives and rolling stock were grouped into an all-Queensland class and numbering system which greatly assisted future identification.

The Cairns Railway passenger carriages were, until fairly recently, well known because of their "vintage" appearance, and such things as open end verandahs, sun shades over the windows, and short wheelbases were commonplace. Whilst this may not have endeared them to passengers in either travelling comfort or appearance, it meant that their continued existence became a useful source of suitable "vintage" carriages for the Queensland Railways "Vintage Train" which was formed in 1965 at the request of the Australian Railway Historical Society Queensland Division, and the train has seen extensive use on historical occasions and at Centenary celebrations, hauled by one of the PB15 class locomotives which were retained in service after full dieselisation for use on special trains.

Over the years a number of the carriages were converted at the Cairns Workshops, some of them being changed from ordinary carriages to vehicles with guard's compartments, fitting lavatories for additional passenger comfort, and some have even seen change in their class designation, e.g. from 1st. to 2nd. or vice versa. The use of travelling post offices in Queensland has never been as extensive as in Great Britain for example, though in the early years of this century, these vans were to be found on a number of trains where the postal men sorted the mail as the train proceeded on its journey. The Cairns Railway was not missed, and between 1910 and 1918, a small van, No. 233, was used on the services to Ravenshoe. There were also two horse boxes (capable of holding only two horses each) which came to the railway new in 1889 from the Queensland Carriage Co. at Nundah (Brisbane) and remained in use until after 1924. The railway also had a number of the small 15'0" long 4-wheel Goods Brake Vans which were a common feature on most Cairns goods train and mixed trains until the mid-1930s. In 1911 the Q.R. took over eight carriages from the Cairns—Mulgrave Tramway and in 1919, two carriages from the Chillagoe Co. Whilst the Chillagoe Co. carriages have now been withdrawn, some of the Tramway carriages built by James Frost & Co. of Ipswich between 1903 and 1911 are still in use in the Q.R. Vintage Train.

The goods rolling stock had very humble beginnings in 1887 and the small number of wagons must have presented serious problems for the fast growing railway in the early days. It was not until 1900 that any significant increase in the stock took place, however from then until 1924, the stock was added to steadily to meet the demands of a growing population and mining and agricultural development. From the table showing the stock disposition, it is possible to assess from the various types of wagon introduced, just where this development was taking place, for example, the increase in timber wagons in 1901-02, the cattle trucks in 1912-13, and the use of insulated and refrigerated vans for such commodities as meat and butter from 1918-19. After the mining boom had reached its peak about 1908, many of the people from these areas drifted to the flourishing sugar cane areas on the coast around Cairns and the growth in this industry is reflected in the arrival of forty-eight FC cane trucks in 1911-12. The cane wagons were usually normal wagons which had the body removed and at each end, two stanchions were placed to keep the long cane stalks in place on the wagon and a ratchet and chain to hold down the load. The reader may wonder at the use of wagons fitted up for firewood traffic, however it must be remembered that in those days domestic fires and the furnaces used in connection with the mining industry relied heavily on wood, coal not being in ready supply and the bulk of it had to be imported from the south. Mt. Mulligan coal helped to relieve this situation from 1915 but there was still a dependence on wood for many years after that, especially in the outback areas.

There were also some interesting wagons to be found in the area. Taking them in alphabetical order of their class codes, the first of these were the CC vans. These were large bogie vans with six doors, with a window in each, on each side of the wagon. Internally they were completely open, but at times of heavy passenger traffic, such as the occasion of the annual railway employees picnic, it was possibly to fit long plank seats across the vans, thus making them into a sort of carriage, and although possibly uncomfortable, sufficed for the occasion. The two Cairns CC vans were converted into CCBs by the addition of a guard's compartment in 1907, but these were transferred away to the main Southern and Central Division almost immediately. A number of other wagons were similarly converted, for example, the HB, KB and UB wagons, the idea being that by fitting a guard's compartment to the wagon, it would not be necessary to haul a special brake van, and thus be a saving in the tare weight of the train, especially at the time of their introduction in 1907 when the load of a B15 on the Cairns Range was only 130 tons. The fact that the wagon, being the brake van for the train, could not be left on an intermediate siding, lessened their practicability, except in the case of cattle trucks which could be run as whole train for the complete journey, and many of them were therefore re—converted to ordinary goods wagons from the mid-1920s. Other interesting wagons were the HC, later HX, coke wagons which were no doubt used in connection with the mining industry, the timber wagons of Q, S and SG classes, showing the importance of this industry, the well known T class 4-wheel ballast wagons, which constituted the largest class of wagon prior to 1924 with a maximum of 212 in 1922-23, and the Explosives Vans, of which there were eight—a large number for such a small railway, and again, no doubt due to the mining industry.

The service vehicles were always an important part of any railway system, and they were no less so at Cairns. The familiar water tank, or "gin" as it is more commonly termed in railway parlance, did not see extensive use until after the Q.G.R. had taken over the Chillagoe Co. lines in 1919.These lines covered large distances over comparatively dry areas, and the use of the gin was often a necessity, not only for engine purposes, but also for the domestic use of railway employees, especially the permanent way gangs. The breakdown van has an important use in the breakdown train being used to transport all manner of equipment from tools to spare couplings, buffers and wheels or the like. A number of open wagons were also used in the train to transport the more bulky items of the breakdown gang's "bits and pieces" such as spare bogies, timber packing, jacks and chains. The Cairns travelling crane was a small eight—wheel 7-ton hand—operated type, built by Dempster & Sons of Halifax, England in 1887. It continued in use for the whole of the railway's isolated existence, and for many years thereafter. Similar cranes were still in service until comparatively recently, although the introduction of heavier locomotives and rolling stock restricted their use to only light duties.

After the opening of the North Coast Line, at first there was little change in the rolling stock position, but as the years passed, other types of carriages and wagons, previously unknown in Cairns, began to find their way to this area, though the bulk of the goods stock used still reflected the agricultural, and, to a lesser extent by this time, mining development which was taking place. In the 1920s there was an increasing awareness of the tourist potential of the tropical areas of North Queensland and although progress to cater for this demand was somewhat hampered by the Depression in the 1930s, plans continued apace, and from 1929, the route from Brisbane to Cairns became known as the "Sunshine Route", an apt description. This was followed in 1935 by the introduction of the famous "Sunshine Express" which soon became well known throughout Australia and to a certain extent overseas. For this new service, three carriage sets of a completely new design were built at the Ipswich Railway Workshops in 1935 comprising first and second class sitting and sleeping cars and parlour cars. Two kitchen cars, later converted to dining cars, were also provided, but only operated between Rockhampton and Mackay. The new "Sunshine" cars were all of similar external appearance with varnished exterior, and polished interior panelling, whilst their length of 52'6" and tare weight of 27 to 30 tons made them some of the largest carriages then operating in Queensland. It is interesting to note that this train was the first complete train in Australia to be fitted with roller bearing axles, a feature that was to become important on all new rolling stock, both passenger and goods, in later years.

The "Sunshine Express" wooden carriage sets, strengthened over the years by the addition of new vehicles of similar appearance, and at times of heavy traffic by carriages of different design, continued in regular use on this service until 1953 when Queensland Railways introduced their first air-conditioned train services, and the Brisbane to Cairns service was equipped with new train sets known as the "Sunlander". The special all-steel carriages for this service, in an attractive blue and white livery, were built by Commonwealth Engineering Pty. Ltd. at Rocklea in Brisbane, whilst later additional cars were constructed at the Ipswich Railway Workshops. Like the "Sunshine Express", the new trains had first and second class sitting and sleeping cars, and dining cars, but additional vehicles included power cars (housing the air-conditioning generators), composite first and second class sleeping cars, and luggage and brake vans, all built to the same general outline and giving the trains a most pleasing and attractive appearance. The cars were each 57'4" long and had a tare weight of 30 to 37 tons, making them the heaviest passenger vehicles on Queensland Railways. Until recent years, the air-conditioned carriages have been confined to the "Lander" services but in May and June 1974, the Queensland Symphony Orchestra used a seven-car air-conditioned train on their annual tour of Queensland, and this included a trip from Cairns to Atherton and return, the first time that the a/c cars worked up the Cairns Range. Later in the same year, a special five car Royal Train including six of the a/c cars was used to convey the King and Queen of Persia from Cairns to Kuranda during their visit to North Queensland.

Before leaving the rolling stock, mention must be made of four special carriages which were unique to the Cairns area, and to the author's knowledge, the only vehicles of their type to operate in Australia. They were known as the "Grandstand" cars and were provided specifically for the use of tourists on the train to Kuranda, highlighting the importance placed on this fast—growing industry in the North. The carriages were first class and had a capacity of 42 passengers. They were 45'1" long and had a tare weight of 20 tons 5cwt., and were numbered 506, 507, 533 and 534. Nos. 506 and 507 had originally been built at Ipswich in 1909-10 as second class lavatory sitting carriages with open end verandahs and sun shades over the windows, whilst Nos. 533 and 534 were built at Ipswich in 1909 of identical exterior design, but fitted internally as composite first and second class sitting carriages. In 1936, Nos. 506, 507 and 533 were taken to Ipswich Railway Workshops and completely rebuilt with twelve 3'6" scenic glass windows along one side of the carriage, a lavatory at one end, and two rows of longitudinal tiered seating, thus affording passengers an unrestricted view of the excellent scenery encountered on the climb up the Cairns Range. No. 507 was also fitted with a small announcers cabinet at one end and all cars were fitted with a public address system so that the accompanying guide could draw passengers attention to points of interest and provide a running commentary on the trip. The cars were normally run in a three—car set, with an additional conventional carriage (normally 1st. class clerestory roof lavatory car No. 440, also fitted with public address equipment, built in 1902), provided as necessary, known as the "Grandstand Train", and proved so popular that in 1938, a further "Grandstand" carriage had to be provided, and

B15 Con. class No. 312 heads slowly across Stoney Creek bridge in 1936 with the "Grandstand Train". The leading carriage is No. 507, built in 1936.

(Late K.J.C. Rogers, courtesy G. Bond)

Above: "Grandstand" carriages Nos. 506, 507 and 508 pose for their photo in Mayne Jct. yard, Brisbane, in 1936 with B18¼ class 4-6-2 No. 23 and a mail brake van before heading north to begin duty on the Cairns Range.
(Queensland Railways)

Below: The interior of "Grandstand" 1st. class carriage No. 507 showing the comfortable tiered seating and scenic windows which made the cars ideal for passengers to enjoy the scenic beauty of the train ride up the Cairns Range to Kuranda.
(Queensland Railways)

No. 534 was converted for this purpose. The service continued until the Second World War stopped all tourist activities and it was withdrawn. The carriages were converted into much-needed ambulance cars and included in one of the Queensland Railways ambulance trains. After the War, all four vehicles were reconverted, but unfortunately to conventional carriages. In recent years, North Queensland had again experienced a tourist "boom" and in 1975 those responsible for tourist development were beginning to appreciate the potential of reintroducing the "Grandstand" carriages. Hopefully this will take place and the traveller will again be able to view the scenery of the Range train journey in this unique way. It is interesting to note that the current Tourist Train carriage set which operates to Kuranda still includes cars 506, 507 and 533, the three original vehicles.

Railmotors

Since 1927, railmotors have played an important part in the operation of the Cairns railway, and in that year, a semi-suburban service was commenced on the North Coast Line to Gordonvale and Aloomba, and a similar service between Cairns and Redlynch. The service had increased to thirty-three journeys per week on these runs, but by 1967, had reduced to five. From 1931 a railmotor commenced running from Mareeba to Ravenshoe, connecting with a steam—hauled passenger train from Cairns at Mareeba, and in 1950 this service became a through railmotor from Cairns to Atherton. A daily return railmotor from Cairns to Mareeba started in 1937, and was extended to Atherton once a week at one time.

Railmotors worked on the Millaa Millaa branch from 1927 and continued until 1963, a year before closure of the line. Additional services were provided in 1934 and were used mainly to haul cream and milk between Atherton and Malanda, where the important North Queensland butter factory is situated. To cater for the local population, a weekly shoppers service was provided from the Mt. Molloy—Rumula branch from 1950 and continued until the line closed in 1964.

On the ex-Chillagoe Co. lines, a railmotor service was provided between Mareeba and Dimbulah from 1959 to 1964, however there is no record of a regular service having been provided on either the Mt. Mulligan or Mt. Garnet branches, although no doubt railmotors did work onto these lines on special occasions. From 1950 to 1958, a monthly shoppers service was provided by railmotors to Cairns from both the Forsayth line and Chillagoe line. As related elsewhere, in 1927 the Forsayth line was extensively damaged by floods and because of damage done to the track, it was not possible to operate steam locomotives beyond Ootan, 8 miles from Almaden. Although their haulage powers were extremely limited, railmotors were allocated to the section from Almaden to Forsayth and worked all services from 1927 to 1939 when the first diesel mechanical locomotive was placed in service. In 1950 steam locomotive operation was extended to Mt. Surprise, and as the diesel mechanical fleet was increased, the railmotors were withdrawn from the services.

For the first thirty years that the Cairns and associated services ran, they were operated almost entirely by the 45 h.p. A.E.C. cars and one 100 h.p. A.E.C car (later converted to a 102

Railmotor RM 53 heads a well loaded suburban peak service into Cairns station from Aloomba in 1960.
(Late R. Tonkies, courtesy J. Knowles)

h.p. diesel). The 100 h.p. vehicle was used to haul up to three railmotor trailers on the busier runs and therefore provided up to 175 somewhat cramped seats. From the late 1950s, more 102 h.p. cars came to be used, and the last 45 h.p. units ran about 1960. Gradually the 102 h.p. cars were also replaced, firstly by the 1800 class, and later the 2000 class railmotors, and by the mid-1960s, they were covering all remaining railmotor services. On the busier runs, some of the railmotor journeys would be operated by a PB15 or B15Con. steam engine hauling up to three or four carriages. This was particularly so when there were insufficient railmotors available and during the sugar cane season to assist in the working of this traffic. On occasions, one of the 153 h.p. diesel mechanical locos would work on the local Cairns services to either Redlynch or Aloomba prior to, or after servicing or overhaul at the Cairns Workshops.

The trailer car towers over Railmotor RM 59 as it heads out of Gordonvale on a run to Aloomba in 1960.
(Late R. Tonkies, courtesy J. Knowles)

Two early views showing the scenic splendour of the Cairns Range. The upper scene shows the Barron Gorge about 1912 with the railway located near the top of the gorge on the left. The lower scene shows Stoney Creek falls and bridge about 1900 with the creek in full flood.

(Both J. Knowles Collection)

Above: C17 class 4-8-0 No. 859 heads a motley collection of rolling stock forming northbound Troop Train No. P500 at Aloomba in 1945.

(J. Buckland)

Below: PB15 class 4-6-0 No. 392 prepares to depart from Cairns with a local train for Gordonvale in 1947. Note four different styles of carriage are used.

(J. M. McMillan, J. Buckland Collection)

Appendix 1

CAIRNS RAILWAY—STEAM LOCOMOTIVES—1887 TO 1960

Class.	1887	1888	1889-94	1894-96	1896-98	1898-99	1899-00	1900-01	1901-06	1906-07	1907-09	1909-10	1910-11	1911-12	1912-13	1913-14	1914-16	1916-17	1917-18	1918-19	1919-21
D11½ 0-6-OCT											1	1	1	1	1	1	1	1			
B11 2-6-0		1	1	1										1	1						
B12 2-6-0														3	3	3	3	3	3	3	3a
B13 4-6-0	2	2	2	3	3	4	5	6	6	6	6	6	6	7	7	7	7	7	8	8	8
B15 4-6-0									2	3	4	7	10	11	9	9	9	7	7	6	12
B15Con 4-6-0										1	1	1	1	2	4	4	5	7	7	8	8
PB15 4-6-0																					
AY 2-6-0																					1
BY 2-6-0																					1
C16 4-8-0																					
B14 2-6-0																					

Class.	1921-22	1922-23	1923-24	1924-25	1925-26	1926-27	1927-28	1928-30	1930-31	1931-32	1932-33	1933-34	1934-35	1935-36	1936-37	1937-38	1938-39	1939-41	1941-42	1942-43	1943-44	1944-45
D11½ 0-6-OCT																						
B11 2-6-0																						
B12 2-6-0	3a	1	1	1	1	1																
B13 4-6-0	8	8	8	9	7	6	5	2	2	2	2	2	2	2	1	1	1					
B15 4-6-0	12	10	9	8	6	5	4	3	3	3	3	3										
B15Con 4-6-0	10	14	17	18	20	17	19	23	23	28	29	29	28	28	28	29	28	27	23	27	27	27
PB15 4-6-0						3	1	1	4	5	4	3	4	2	2	2	3	4	4	10	14	16
AY 2-6-0	1	1	1																			
BY 2-6-0	1																					
C16 4-8-0														1	1	1	1	1	1	1	1	1
B14 2-6-0				1	1	1																

Class.	1945-47	1947-49	1949-50	1950-51	1951-52	1952-54	1954-55	1955-57	1957-59	1959-60
B15Con 4-6-0	27	27	22	15	15	14	10	10	8	6
PB15 4-6-0	16	18	18	18	17	18	21	19	19	17
C16 4-8-0	1	1	1	1	2	2			3	3
C17 4-8-0		1	1	1						1

a—two of the three engines out of service awaiting disposal.

Appendix 2

CAIRNS RAILWAY—PASSENGER CARRIAGES—1887 to 1924

Description of Carriage		Code	1887-89	1889-91	1891-92	1892-98	1898-99	1899-00	1900-03	1903-05	1905-06	1906-07	1907-08	1908-09	1909-10	1910-11
1st. Class Lavatory		AL													1	2
1st. Class Lavatory Van	sv	ALV														
Composite Lavatory		CL								1	1	3	6	6	6	6
Composite Lavatory Van	lv	CLV														2
Composite Lavatory Van	sv	CLV								1	1	1	1	1	3	4
Composite Ordinary		CO	2	2	2	2	3	4	4	4	4	4	2	1		
Composite Van	lv	CV			1	2	2	2	3	3	3	3	3	3	3	1
Composite Van	sv	CV							1	1	1	1	2	2	2	2
2nd. Class Ordinary		BO												1	1	1
2nd. Class Lavatory		BL														
Goods Brake Van with 2nd. Compts.		GBV														
Postal Van		TPO														1
4-wheel Goods Brake Van		BV	2	2	2	2	2	3	3	3	4	6	8	8	8	8
4-wheel Horse Box (two stall)		ZGa	2	2	2	2	2	2	2	2	2	2	2	2	2	2
Railmotor		RM														
Railmotor Tractor-Goods only		RT														
Railmotor Trailer-Goods only		-														

a—ZG code applied to Horse Boxes in 1910-1911.

sv—fitted with small guard's compartment.
lv—fitted with large guard's compartment.

Description of Carriage		Code	1911-12	1912-13	1913-14	1914-15	1915-16	1916-17	1917-18	1918-19	1919-20	1920-21	1921-22	1922-23	1923-24
1st. Class Lavatory		AL	2	2	2	3	3	3	3	3	3	3	4	5	5
1st. Class Lavatory Van	sv	ALV		1	1	1	1	1	1	1	1	1	1	1	1
Composite Lavatory		CL	8	7	7	7	9	9	9	9	9	9	9	9	11
Composite Lavatory Van	lv	CLV	2	2	2	2	2	2	2	2	3	3	3	3	3
Composite Lavatory Van	sv	CLV	7	8	8	8	8	8	8	9	9	9	9	9	9
Composite Ordinary		CO	4	4	4	4	2	2	2	2	2	2	2		
Composite Van	lv	CV	1	1	1	1	1	1	1	1	2	2	2	2	2
Composite Van	sv	CV	2	1	1	1	1	1	1						
2nd. Class Ordinary		BO	3	3	3	3	3	3	3	3	3	3	3	2	2
2nd. Class Lavatory		BL	3	2	2	2	2	2	2	2	2	2	3	4	7
Goods Brake Van with 2nd. Compts.		GBV								1	1	1	1	1	1
Postal Van		TPO	1	1	1	1	1	1	1						
4-wheel Goods Brake Van		BV	10	10	10	10	10	10	10	10	11	11	11	11	10
4-wheel Horse Box (two stall)		ZGa	2	2	2	2	2	2	2	2	2	2	2	2	2
Railmotor		RM									4	5	5	4	4
Railmotor Tractor-Goods only		RT												1	1
Railmotor Trailer-Goods only		-												2	2

CAIRNS RAILWAY—PASSENGER CARRIAGES—1935

Description	No.	Tare Wt.	Compts. 1st.	Compts. 2nd.	Passgrs. 1st.	Passgrs. 2nd.	Body Length	Overall Length	Running Numbers
1st. Lavatory	1	11t. 0c.	1	-	30	-	25' 8"	31' 7"	AL 265
1st. Lavatory	1	11t.10c.	2	-	32	-	30' 0"	39' 5"	AL 194
1st. Lavatory	1	24t.10c.	1	-	48	-	45' 0"	52'11"	AL 454
1st. Lavatory Brake	1	14t.11c.	1	-	24	-	34'11"	41' 3"	ALV 266
Composite Lavatory	2	12t.10c.	1	1	16	24	34' 0"	42' 5"	CL 287, 288
Composite Lavatory	1	12t. 0c.	1	1	12	22	30' 0"	39' 5"	CL 187
Composite Lavatory	1	16t. 0c.	3	3	24	30	45' 0"	48' 3"	CL 337
Composite Lavatory	2	14t.10c.	1	1	16	32	39' 0"	48' 5"	CL 466, 467
Composite Lavatory	1	13t.10c.	1	1	20	30	39' 0"	48' 5"	CL 830
Comp. Lavatory Brake	2	14t.10c.	2	2	16	20	45' 1"	48' 5"	CLV 328, 329
Comp. Lavatory Brake	1	14t.10c.	1	3	16	30	42' 2"	48' 6"	CLV 415
Comp. Lavatory Brake	1	14t.10c.	1	1	10	30	39' 0"	48' 5"	CLV 197
Comp. Lavatory Brake	6	21t. 5c.	1	1	14	22	45' 0"	52'11"	CLV 504, 505, 532, 732, 733, 734
Composite	2	8t.15c.	1	4	13	35	26' 3"	34' 6"	C 826, 827
Composite	1	11t.13c.	1	1	12	28	30' 1"	39' 6"	C 828
Composite	1	11t.13c.	1	1	16	24	30' 1"	39' 6"	C 829
Composite Brake	1	12t.10c.	1	2	8	20	37' 4"	40' 8"	CV 205
Composite Brake	1	13t. 0c.	1	1	12	32	39' 0"	48' 3"	CV 199
2nd. Class	3	8t. 0c.	-	5	-	60	25' 3"	34' 6"	B 823, 824, 825
2nd. Class Lavatory	1	10t.10c.	-	1		32	25' 7"	31' 7"	BL 267
2nd. Class Lavatory	1	11t. 0c.	-	2	-	36	30' 0"	39' 5"	BL 189
Postal Van	1	12t.19c.	-	-	-	-	33' 0"	36' 5"	233
Goods Brake Vans 4-wheel.	10	7t. 0c.	-	-	-	-	15' 0"	18' 5"	2, 4, 7, 27, 28, 35 38, 43, 71, 72

CAIRNS RAILWAY—PASSENGER CARRIAGES—1916

Description	Running Numbers	Guard's Compt.
1st. Lavatory	AL 265, 194, 454	
1st. Lavatory Brake	ALV 266	small
Composite Lavatory	CL 287, 288, 187, 337,466, 467, 830	
Composite Lavatory Brake	CLV 328, 329	large
Composite Lavatory Brake	CLV 415, 197, 504, 505, 532, 732, 733, 734	small
Composite	C 826, 827, 828, 829	
Composite Brake	CV 205	large
Composite Brake	CV 199	small
2nd. Class	B 823, 824, 825	
2nd. Class Lavatory	BL 267, 189	
Postal Van	233	
Goods Brake Van (4-wheel)	2, 4, 7, 27, 28, 35, 38, 43, 71, 72	

Appendix 3

CAIRNS RAILWAY—GOODS ROLLING STOCK—1887 to 1924

Description	Code	Wheels	1887	1888	1888-89	1889-90	1890-91	1891-93	1893-94	1894-97	1897-98	1898-99	1899-00	1900-01
Covered Goods Van	A	4											4	4
Insulated Butter Van	ABG	4G												
Louvred Van	ALG	4G												
Covered Goods Van	C	8	6	6	6	9	9	9	9	9	9	9	27	27
Convertible Goods/Passenger Van	CC	8	2	2	2	2	2	2	2	2	2	2	2	2
Convert. Goods/Pass Van/Brake	CCB	8												
Louvred Cream Van	CLC	8												
Insulated Frozen Meat Van	CM	8												
High Sided Goods Wagon	DF	4											10	10
Low Sided Goods Wagon	F	4										4	4	3
Cane Wagon	FC	4												
Low Sided Goods Wagon	FG	4G												
Low Sided Goods Wagon	H	8										6	17	17
Low Sided Goods Wagon/Brake	HB	8												
Coke Wagon	HX	8												
Cattle Truck	IC	4				2	2	2	2	2	2	2	2	2
Cattle Truck	ICG	4G												
Cattle Truck	K	8												8
Cattle Truck/Brake	KB	8												
Sheep Truck	L	4												
Sheep and Pig Truck	MGP	4G												
Platform (Flat) Wagon	P	8				1	1	1	1	1	1	1	13	13
Timber Wagon	Q	4						12	12	2	2	2	2	2
Timber Wagon	S	8	6	6	6	6	6	12	12	12	18	24	34	34
Timber Wagon	SG	4G												
Ballast Wagon	T	4	12	30	30	30	30	18	17	17	17	17	17	17
Ballast Wagon	U	8												
Ballast Wagon/Brake	UB	8												
Steel Ballast Hopper Wagon	VTS	4												
Explosives Van	-	4							1	1	1	3	3	3
Water Tank (Gin)	-	4							1	1	1	1	3	2
Breakdown Van	-	8												
Travelling Crane (7-ton)	-	8	1	1	1	1	1	1	1	1	1	1	1	1

G—These wagons are fitted with a 4-wheel Grover's Bogie.
HX—Originally these wagons were coded HC, changed to HX in 1914.
T—Some wagons were later fitted for carrying cane and coded TC. Some also fitted for firewood traffic.

Code	*Wheels*	1901-02	1902-04	1904-05	1905-06	1906-07	1907-08	1908-09	1909-10	1910-11	1911-12	1912-13	1913-14	1914-15	1915-16	1916-17	1917-18	1918-19	1919-20	1920-21	1921-22	1922-23	1923-24
A	4	4	4	4	4	4	4	4	4	4	8	8	8	8	8	8	8	8	8	8	8	8	8
ABG	4G														8	8	8	2	2	2	2	2	2
ALG	4G					2	6	6	6	6	6	6	6	6	6	6	6	6	6	6	6	6	6
C	8	37	37	37	49	49	49	49	49	49	49	49	49	49	49	49	49	47	47	47	47	47	45
CC	8	2	2	2	2		8	8	8	13	13	13	13	13	13	13	13	13	13	13	13	13	12
CCB	8					2																	
CLC	8																	2	2	2	2	2	2
CM	8																4	6	6	6	18	18	18
DF	4	10	10	10	10	10	10	10	10	10	10	10	10	10	10	10	10	10	10	10	10	10	10
F	4	3	4	4	4	4	4	4	4	4	29	29	29	29	30	30	30	30	30	30	30	30	29
FC	4										48	48	48	48	48	48	48	48	48	45	48	28	58
FG	4G																		10	35	35	35	35
H	8	47	47	57	57	57	52	52	72	72	163	176	176	176	176	176	176	176	176	176	173	183	192
HB	8						5	5	5	5	5	5	5	5	5	5	5	5	5	5	5	5	5
HX	8						10	10	10	10	10	10	10	10					10	10	10	10	10
IC	4	2	2	2	2	2	2	2	2	2	1	1	1	1				2	2	2	2	2	2
ICG	4G										2	2	2	2	2	2	2	2	2	2	2	2	2
K	8	8	8	8	8	8	8	8	8	8	8	22	26	26	26	26	26	26	35	35	35	35	34
KB	8											2	2	2	2	2	2	2	3	3	3	3	3
L	4																			2	2	2	2
MGP	4G											2	2	2	2	2	2	2	2	2	2	2	2
P	8	13	13	13	2	2	2	2	2	2	2	2	2	2	2	2	2	2	2	2	2	2	2
Q	4	2	2	2	2	2	2	2	2	2	2	2	2	2	2	2	2	2	2	2	2	2	2
S	8	73	73	73	72	72	80	92	110	112	129	129	129	129	129	131	131	131	131	131	131	141	146
SG	4G																						5
T	4	17	17	17	17	49	49	59	59	59	76	76	76	127	130	130	137	137	193	192	192	212	208
U	8				5	5	5	5	5	26	26	26	26	26	26	26	26	26	26	26	26	26	25
UB	8									1	1	1	1	1	1	1	1	1	1	1	1	1	1
VST	4							20	20	20	20	20	30	30	30	30	30	30	30	33	9	15	15
-	4	3	3	3	6	6	6	8	8	8	8	8	8	8	8	8	8	8	8	8	8	8	7
-	4	2	2	2	2	2	2	2	2	2	2	2	3	2	2	2	2	2	6	7	7	7	11
-	8									1	1	1	1	1	1	1	1	1	1	1	1	1	1
-	8	1	1	1	1	1	1	1	1	1	1	1	1	1	1	1	1	1	1	1	1	1	1

IC—Originally coded I, changed to CI in 1896, IC in 1907.
C—One wagon later fitted with refrigerated space.
H—Some wagons later had no sides but ends and fitted for carrying cane and coded HC.

OPENING AND CLOSING DATES OF LINES IN THE CAIRNS DIVISION

Section	Length	Total	Opened	Closed
Cairns-Ravenshoe Main Line				
Cairns to Redlynch	7.37m.		8/10/1887	Still open.
Redlynch to Myola	16.31m.		15/ 6/1891	Still open.
Myola to Biboohra	17.58m.		2/ 1/1893	Still open.
Biboohra to Mareeba	5.35m.		1/ 8/1893	Still open.
Mareeba to Atherton	21.26m.		10/ 8/1903	Still open.
Atherton to Herberton	14.92m.		20/10/1910	Still open.
Herberton to Tumoulin	17.17m.		31/ 7/1911	Still open.
Tumoulin to Ravenshoe	4.50m.		11/12/1916	Still open.
Cairns Wharf Branch	0.98m.	105.44m.	-/10/1887	Still open.
Mt.Molloy-Rumula Branch				
Biboohra to Mt. Molloy	20.0m.		1/ 3/1917	30/4/1964.
Mt. Molloy to Rumula	7.10m.	27.1m.	7/12/1926	
Millaa Millaa Branch				
Tolga to Yungaburra	10.29m.		15/ 3/1910	30/6/1964.
Yungaburra to Kureen	7.20m.		18/10/1910	
Kureen to Malanda	1.48m.		20/12/1910	
Malanda to Jaggan	4.57m.		22/10/1915	
Jaggan to Tarzali	3.62m.		15/ 9/1916	
Tarzali to Millaa Millaa	9.35m.	36.51m.	19/12/1921	
Cairns-Mulgrave Shire Tramway				
Cairns to Mulgrave	14.0m.		-/ 5/1897	Taken over by the QGR 1/7/1911. Still open.
Mulgrave to Aloomba	3.7m.		-/ 8/1898	
Aloomba to Harvey's Creek	13.0m.		-/ 8/1903	
Harvey's Creek to Babinda	7.0m.	37.7m.	-/ 2/1910	
North Coast Line				
Babinda to Pawngilly	4.71m.		9/12/1912	Still open.
Pawngilly to Daradgee	8.95m.	13.66m.	13/ 9/1919	Still open.
Chillagoe Co. Main Line				
Mareeba to Lappa Junction	55.8m.		1/10/1900	Taken over by the QGR 20/6/1919. Still open.
Lappa Junction to Chillagoe	36.45m.		-/ 6/1901	
Chillagoe to Mungana	10.63m.	102.88m.	2/ 8/1901	
Mt. Mulligan Branch				
Dimbulah to Mt. Mulligan	29.8m.		7/ 4/1915	1/7/1958.
Mt. Garnet Branch				
Lappa Junction to Ord	16.03m.		16/11/1901	Taken over by the QGR 23/12/1914. Closed 1/7/1963
Ord to Mt. Garnet	16.65m.	32.68m.	29/ 4/1902	
Forsayth Branch				
Almaden to Forsayth	142.32m.	142.32m.	-/ 8/1908	Taken over by the QGR 20/6/1919. Still open.
Stannary Hills and Irvinebank Tramway (2'0" Gauge—not part of the QGR).				
Boonmoo to Stannary Hills	14.0m.		9/ 5/1902	-/12/1936.
Stannary Hills to Rocky Bluff	7.0m.		18/11/1902	-/ -/1926.
Irvinebank Jct. to Irvinebank	13.5m.	34.5m.	29/ 1/1907	-/12/1936.

Two very different forms of motive power. PB 15 class No. 559 and two of the Diesel Mechanical 2-6-0 locos built specially for the Etheridge Railway to Forsayth, at Mt. Surprise in 1963.

(E. Ward)

Bibliography And Acknowledgements.

The author acknowledges the assistance of the following publications:- "Sunshine Route Jubilee" by John Armstrong and John Kerr.
"3'6" Gauge Locomotives of the Queensland Railways" by John Armstrong.
"The Railways of Queensland—A lineside Guide" by John Knowles.
Commissioner for Railways Annual Reports in the A.R.H.S. Qld. Div. Archives.
Queensland Railways Rolling Stock Diagrams in the A.R.H.S. Qld. Div. Archives.
"Sunshine Express" Journal of the A.R.H.S. Qld. Div., various issues.
"The Bulletin" Journal of the Australian Railway Historical Society; in particular the following issues and articles:-
Nos. 234 & 239 - "Railways of the Cairns District" by the late C.C. Singleton.
No. 187 - "The Construction of the Cairns—Mareeba Railway" by G. Smith.
No. 362 - "The Rail Motors of the Queensland Railways" by John Knowles.
No. 395 - "Distribution of Queensland Trains by Direction, Code and Number" by John Kerr.
No. 420 - "Provincial Suburban Trains in Queensland" by John Knowles.
No. 275 - "Wagon Brakevans of the Queensland Railways" by John Knowles.
No. 413 - "The Cairns—Mulgrave Tramway" by John Armstrong and Gerry Verhoeven.
"Light Railways" - Journal of the Light Railway Research Society of Australia.
Particular thanks are extended to George Robinson and Ted Ward who both willingly placed at the authors disposal their extensive information on the Cairns Railway. Thanks are also extended to the following people who have assisted in a number of ways with information and photographs:- John Armstrong, A.R.H.S. Queensland Division, George Bond, John Buckland, Cairns Historical Society, Cyril Henshaw, John Knowles, Wal Larsen, F. Robson, John Southern, Ken Winney.

Most non-railway enthusiasts books which deal with the Cairns Railway and the early history of the Cairns area are now, regretably, out of print, however they are recommended, and readers may care to enquire into their availability with their local library:-
"Early Days of Cairns" by J.W. Collinson.
"More about Cairns" by J.W. Collinson.
"Tropic Coasts and Tablelands" by J. W. Collinson.
"Northmost Australia" by Dr. R.I. Jack.
"Round the Compass in Australia" by G. Parker.
"Early Days in North Queensland" by Edward Palmer.
"Climbing the Ladder" by F.T. Wimble.
"Spinafex and Wattle" by Inspector R. Johnstone.

A resident at Cairns shed for a number of years was B15 Con. class No. 299, the first main line engine built by Walkers Ltd. of Maryborough, in 1897. Seen here shunting the yard in 1964. The engine is now preserved in Maryborough. *(E. Ward)*

The Australian Railway Historical Society was formed in Sydney in 1933 and now has Divisions incorporated in all States.

Membership is open to persons over the age of fifteen years who are interested in railways, and the society's activities include publication of information concerning past and present railway history, production of recordings, promotion of train excursions, the latter often hauled by steam locomotives specially retained by arrangement with the various Australian railway administrations, while active research and compilation of authentic records of our railway network is encouraged.

An illustrated monthly Bulletin is produced containing many excellent articles on various railway and tramway subjects throughout Australia. Each Division, in addition, publishes its own supplementary news magazine which generally covers current events. The Society as a whole has been involved with several preservation projects, including locomotive museums at Redbank, Queensland; North Williamstown, Victoria; Mile End, South Australia; and at Bassendean in Western Australia.

Back Cover Top: The most attractive station in Queensland—Kuranda

(R. Deskins)

Back Cover Bottom: Surprise Creek Bridge in July 1966 with B15Con. class 4-6-0 No. 306 crossing on an ARHS special to Kuranda.

(R. Deskins)